My Dear Mr McCourt

My Dear Mr McCourt

Eugene McCague

Gill & Macmillan

Gill & Macmillan Ltd
Hume Avenue, Park West, Dublin 12
with associated companies throughout the world
www.gillmacmillan.ie

© Eugene McCague 2009

978 07171 4658 1

Index compiled by Rachel Pierce, Verba Editing House
Print origination by TypeIT, Dublin
Printed and bound in Great Britain by the MPG Books Group

This book is typeset in 11pt New Baskerville on 15pt.
The paper used in this book comes from the wood pulp of managed forests. For every tree felled, at least one tree is planted, thereby renewing natural resources.

All rights reserved.
No part of this publication may be copied, reproduced or transmitted in any form or by any means, without permission of the publishers.

A CIP catalogue record for this book is available from the British Library.

5 4 3 2 1

To Marie-Christine

Contents

Acknowledgments		1
Introduction		3
Chapter 1	Early Life	5
Chapter 2	Federation of Irish Manufacturers, 1944–9	14
Chapter 3	Industrial Development Authority, 1949–51	33
Chapter 4	P.J. Carroll & Co., 1951–9, and Hunter Douglas, 1959–62	56
Chapter 5	RTÉ, 1963–8	72
Chapter 6	United Distillers, 1968–78	126
Chapter 7	Irish Steel, 1974–86	152
Chapter 8	The Non-Executive Director	167
Chapter 9	A Reflection	177
Appendix	Address by Kevin McCourt to the Institute of Directors in Ireland, 12 November 1986	188
References		200
Selected Bibliography		214
Index		216

Acknowledgments

I am indebted to many people who gave me support, encouragement and advice in writing this book. In particular, I would like to thank Kevin McCourt's family—his children, Pamela, Declan, Germaine and Deirdre, and his grandchildren—for sharing with me their memories of Kevin and for giving me access to his papers.

My research into Kevin's career afforded me the opportunity to meet with many of his friends and colleagues and hear their recollections not just of Kevin but of the business environment in which he operated for nearly half a century. I also received great professional encouragement from historians who, as ever, were only too willing to give their time in assisting an enthusiastic amateur. I owe particular thanks to Mary Banotti, Richard Burrows, Gay Byrne, Liam Coughlan, Aleck Crichton, Laurence Crowley, Dermot Desmond, David Dillon, Tom Garvin, Tom Hardiman, Pat Heneghen, John Horgan, Justin Keating, Howard Kilroy, Muiris MacConghail, Neil McCann, Noel McComish, James O'Dwyer, Frank O'Reilly, Turlough O'Sullivan, Tom Quinn, Fran Rooney, Clem Ryan, Gene Savage, Sheamus Smith, David Sheehy, Paula Somers, Dr Michael Smurfit and Dr T.K. Whitaker.

I received great assistance from Therese Broy, Librarian at Arthur Cox, and from her colleagues, as well as from Seamus Heferty of the UCD Archives and the staff at the National Archive and National Library. The excellent *Irish Times* Archive became available online at just the right time. I was given generous access to the records of the RTÉ Authority.

As with my previous book, the burden of typing and re-typing interminable drafts fell on my secretary, Joan Saunders, whose support was, as always, invaluable.

My wife, Marie-Christine, to whom this book is dedicated, and my children, Ellen, Eoin and Ronan, put up with the disruptions caused by my research with customary good humour and provided me with constant support, encouragement and refreshments.

Eugene McCague
February 2009

Introduction

Kevin McCourt maintained a unique and fascinating personal archive, lovingly filed away in over one hundred bound volumes. The archive, of which he was rightly very proud, includes business papers, board minutes, copies of speeches and newspaper articles interspersed with family photographs and correspondence with children, grandchildren and friends.

A conversation with Declan McCourt on how best to preserve the archive led to Declan giving me access to Kevin's papers for the purpose of writing a memoir of his father. What started out some years ago as an attempt to chart a summary of Kevin's career for the benefit of his family has ended in the publication of this book, which I hope will serve to bring the contribution made by Kevin McCourt to Irish business to the attention of a wider audience.

As might be expected, Kevin's papers are more detailed and comprehensive in relation to some parts of his career than others. Some of the positions he held, most notably that of Director General of RTÉ, attracted great public attention at the time and have already been written about on many occasions, thus making my task much easier. By contrast, Kevin kept very few papers from his time at P.J. Carrolls. I found it difficult to supplement the limited information in the archive in relation to this period with other source materials or interviews. While his time in Holland and London with Hunter Douglas did have a significant influence on his subsequent career, I have not dwelled on this period to any extent because my focus was on Kevin's role in Irish business.

The title of the book—*My Dear Mr McCourt*—is taken from a comment made to Kevin by Seán Lemass, quoted in Chapter 3.

I only hope that I have done some justice to a very worthy subject, a man I had the privilege of meeting on only a few occasions but who meant so much to so many people.

Chapter 1

Early Life

Kevin Colum McCourt was born in Tralee, County Kerry, on 14 April 1915. Although he lived nearly all of his life in Dublin after his family moved there when he was nine years old, he always saw himself as a Kerryman. In fact, his Kerry background was by chance. His father John (Seán) was born in May 1886 in Banbridge, County Down, the second eldest in a family of eleven children born to Charles McCourt, a linen lapper, and his wife Mary (née O'Brien). The McCourt family were believed to be descendants of Séamus Dall MacCuarta, a blind poet of the seventeenth/eighteenth century who was noted for his political verse during the days of the Penal Laws.

From his earliest days Seán McCourt was a fervent Irish nationalist, openly active in both the Gaelic Athletic Association and the Gaelic League—two organisations at the heart of a growing new Irish nationalism. Banbridge was a predominantly Unionist town and in 1912, as tensions rose in Ulster as a result of the Home Rule Bill of that year, Seán McCourt was given a choice: either leave Banbridge immediately or his father would lose his job in the local linen factory. Seán collected his girlfriend, Mary Christina (Minnie) Small, on the way and headed for Dublin, where they got married. The couple then moved on to Tralee, where he secured a job as a clerk with the Congested Districts Board. Speaking of his late father Kevin once remarked that 'In the same situation today, he'd probably just have been shot. But he went as far as he could with the money available—to Tralee.'[1]

In later life, Kevin recorded that 'as a child, teenager, adult, I never heard my father refer to his GAA and Irish language activities, nor of his returning to the scenes of former glories.'[2] Seán McCourt's contribution to the development of the GAA in County Down was significant but, as with his involvement with the Irish language movement, he had a tendency to court controversy in those early years.

In the spring of 1903, aged just seventeen, Seán was the principal mover behind the formation of the first hurling club in Banbridge—Clann na Banna—for whom he played at centrefield. Walking to their first match against a team from Newry, they were set upon by a group opposed to the playing of games on the Sabbath and a riot ensued. For their next match, an escort of eighty constables was required to see them safely to their destination and onto the field.

McCourt was dissatisfied with the attitude of the GAA towards the developing game in the Northern counties. On receiving an offhand response from the Central Council to a query in relation to the interpretation of a rule, he voiced his annoyance in a letter to the *Leader* newspaper in February 1904. 'Is it not time the Councils took it into their hands to act in a businesslike way?' he asked, and went on:

> Suppose the Gaelic League had treated all the letters they received asking for information as to the rules in order to start a branch as the Provincial Council treated mine – with contempt, or else replied with such a profuse definition of the Rules as I received from Central Council, how far would our National language have penetrated into the country?

How many Branches of the Gaelic League would now be in Ireland? Would there be any? I doubt it, and still, the GAA is the regenerator of our national pastimes. The GAA it is which is to expel and stamp out for ever those foul foreign games that have come into this land to the almost complete annihilation of our own.[3]

The letter received a sharp rebuke from the Secretary of County Down GAA, who asserted that Seán McCourt's complaint showed 'the truth of the adage – "a little learning is a dangerous thing"… let Mr. McCourt take an active part in the working of the Councils, and not talk or write so much – let him work.'[4] Kevin's father took up the challenge. In 1905 he took over the role of County Secretary and became a delegate to the GAA Central Council.

The Gaelic League was founded in 1893 with the objectives of preserving Irish as the national language of the country and encouraging the study and publication of Irish literature. Seán McCourt's involvement with the Gaelic League in Ballyvarley led to him volunteering to give lessons in the Irish language. He started teaching Irish in a Temperance Hall in October 1903. By the following year he was teaching up to eighty students in a hall in Loughbrickland. His day job was as an apprentice law clerk in a solicitor's firm in Banbridge.

Irish classes and games on Sunday were not universally welcomed. The parish priest of Aghaderg, Dean McPolin, did not view the developments in a positive light and used his Sunday sermons to condemn such practices. On one occasion he declared from the pulpit that he had discovered that 'a party is coming here from Banbridge and gathering a lot of boys and girls late in the evening under the guise of teaching Irish to them. I had a lot of trouble trying to crush the evils that were carried on in the Parish by this fellow in an Irish class.'⁵

Unknown to Dean McPolin, his congregation that day included Seán McCourt, who recorded the offending words in shorthand and promptly commenced slander proceedings against the priest. McCourt claimed that the priest's words impugned his ability to teach Irish and that, following the sermon, he had lost his entire class. McCourt was successful in his action, the court awarding damages against Dean McPolin in the amount of £5.50 plus £5 for witness expenses. The local branch of the Hibernians held a function to raise money to reimburse the priest. While Kevin's father had won the case, his victory did little for the cause of the Irish language movement in the area.

The Ireland into which Kevin McCourt was born in 1915 was a country in the midst of enormous and fundamental change. W.B. Yeats said that after the death of Charles Stuart Parnell in 1891, 'a disillusioned and embittered Ireland turned from parliamentary politics',⁶ with culture in its broadest form partly filling the vacuum. By 1915 a new radicalism was evident, driven to a not insignificant extent by those who had come to the Irish question from the perspective of cultural issues, such as language and literature. The decision by John Redmond not only to pledge Irish support for the British war effort but to commit Irish Volunteers to take part in the war on the British side hastened a split in the Volunteers and the demise of the old Irish Parliamentary Party. Three months after Kevin's birth, the Gaelic League, to which his father had been so committed, was taken over by militant nationalists.

While Kevin had fond memories of his time in Kerry, he also recalled it as a troubled place—'the Black and Tans, shootings, vague ugly things like Ballyseedy'.⁷ This is unsurprising given that his nine years living in Kerry ran from before the Easter

Rising through the War of Independence and the Civil War. In February 1916 Patrick Pearse delivered a lecture in Tralee on 'The Nature of Freedom'. His real reason for visiting Kerry was to give the local head of the Irish Republican Brotherhood (IRB) the confidential information that the Rising was to take place on Easter Monday, and that a shipload of arms from Germany was due at Fenit pier on Easter Sunday night. As things transpired, the shipment of arms arrived in Kerry a few days early, leading to the arrest of Roger Casement, who was held in the barracks in Tralee, 'a brief stop off on the way to the inevitable gallows in London'.[8]

The outbreak of Civil War in 1922 was keenly felt in Tralee. In August 1922, 450 officers and men of the Dublin Guards, supporters of the Provisional Government, sailed into Tralee Bay on the *Lady Wicklow*. There followed intense battles between the Dublin Guards and the Republican forces through the streets of the town.

Few events in the Civil War were as controversial as the one recalled by Kevin over fifty years later—the events at Ballyseedy, on 7 March 1923, when eight Republican prisoners who had been held in the Tralee workhouse were killed by a concealed trigger mine. The official account was that the prisoners had been brought to the area to remove an obstruction, comprising a barricade of stones built on the roadway at Ballyseedy Bridge, and that they were killed when the concealed mine exploded. Another version of events suggested that, in retaliation for the murder of five Free State officers a few days earlier, the prisoners were brought to Ballyseedy, were bound hand and foot and roped together in a circle with their backs to a log and some loose stones, under which a mine was placed.[9]

Later in life Kevin also told of how, as a child, he had seen Michael Collins attend Mass in Tralee and witnessed him removing his gun from his belt before going up for Communion.

Given his open espousal of the nationalist cause, at least on cultural issues, while in Banbridge, it would not be unreasonable to have assumed that Seán McCourt would have involved himself in the new nationalism that was taking hold while he and his family lived in Tralee. Whether he was disillusioned with the manner in which the Gaelic League had been taken over, or whether he was focussed on providing for his young family, there is no evidence that he played any active part in the turbulent developments that followed the 1916 Rising. He did, however, retain his passionate interest in the Irish language and the McCourt home was Irish-speaking. Kevin recalled many Irish-speaking visitors arriving at the house, including the legendary Dingle native Patrick Sugrue, who, as 'an Seabhac', was a leading figure in Irish literary circles, later serving as a member of the Irish Senate. He would arrive at the McCourt house 'on a great old-fashioned motor-bike like the one T.E. Lawrence used to ride'.[10]

At the age of three Kevin was, in his own words, 'packed off' to school with the Christian Brothers in Tralee. His brother, Brendan, two years older than him, had steadfastly refused to go to school unless Kevin went with him.

In 1924 Kevin, Brendan and their younger sister, Irene, moved with their parents to live in Dublin. Another brother, Dermot, was born three years later. Seán McCourt took over the running of the Post Office on Sandymount Green. In the back of the Post Office he started a small private library, known as the Argosy Library. Branches were later opened in Dun Laoghaire and Ranelagh.

Kevin continued his education with the Christian Brothers in Dun Laoghaire. One of his teachers was a young man only a few years older than himself, Tomás O'Faoláin (Tommy Phelan). Using the adopted name of Terry O'Sullivan, he would become a successful radio broadcaster and later the writer of the social column in the *Evening Press*, 'Dubliner's Diary', in which Kevin frequently featured. Kevin and O'Sullivan became firm friends in later life.

In September 1930, as he entered fourth year in secondary school, Kevin's parents sent him as a boarder to Blackrock College. Brendan had moved to the school two years earlier on the back of a scholarship awarded on the basis of his Intermediate Certificate results, but he left the summer before Kevin's arrival. Kevin's teachers included Fr John Charles McQuaid, who taught English and who was appointed President of the College in January 1931.

As things transpired, Kevin stayed at Blackrock College for less than one academic year. In April 1931, just as he turned sixteen, his family's modest financial circumstances forced him to leave school. For two years he helped his parents with the Post Office and library. Commenting later on this premature departure from formal education, Kevin remarked: 'It was one of the best things that ever happened. It generated fairly early independence. It is a very good thing to have to earn some contributions to the home you live in.'[11]

In 1933 Kevin got a job with Dublin United Tramways as a junior wages clerk, based in its Summerhill garage. His mother had insisted that he get an office job. He earned 15 shillings a week—enough to allow him to treat himself to a green, three-speed Elswick Hopper bicycle, which he paid for at the rate of two-and-six-pence a week.

Kevin recognised the limitations he faced by not having any formal qualification so, after three years with the Tramway company, he enrolled in a night-time accountancy course at the

College of Commerce in Rathmines. For four years he attended, four nights a week. 'I learned something then that has stayed with me the rest of my life,' he later said. 'If you want to do something, you've got to make sacrifices.'[12] Classes were from 7.00pm until 10.00pm and afterwards he would cycle home, have supper and then study for a correspondence course. Virtually all his free time was given to study. 'It was not an easy thing at that time of life,' he recalled, 'when a young man should be playing cricket and rugby and chasing girls.'[13] Yet he never doubted that it was worth the sacrifice.

He qualified as a certified accountant and a chartered secretary and worked for some time with the firm of Kennedy Crowley and Co. In 1940 he was appointed as accountant and company secretary with C.E. Macauleys, a wool merchant. He recalled:

> For the first time I saw in real life what I had been studying in books. I remember doing my first trial balance, I couldn't ask anyone for advice – I was the qualified man after all. What I learned in Macauleys was that you have to find out things for yourself; if you don't you're a bluffer and sooner or later you'll get caught.[14]

In 1941 Kevin married Margaret (Peggy) McMahon, the youngest of a family of six from Pembroke Road, in Dublin. They had met a few years earlier at the Anglesea Tennis Club in Ballsbridge. Peggy's father was originally from Armagh, her mother from Drumcondra.

Around the same time Kevin thought seriously of joining the British Army and going to fight the Nazis. Not surprisingly, his father was appalled at the notion. Instead he joined the Local Defence Force (LDF). He recalled that at the time there was a great fear of invasion by the Axis powers, but press censorship made it impossible to make any judgment as to whether this fear was well grounded or not. 'The LDF was exciting at first, training three nights a week at Beggar's Bush barracks. We were trained in the use of guns, but nobody gave me a gun – just as well I suppose.'[15]

Kevin and Peggy set up home in a rented flat in 68 Merrion Square. Pamela and Declan were born while they lived there. They later bought a house in Shankill, which they named Clonmore, after Clonmore Terrace in Tralee, where Kevin had lived. Germaine and Deirdre were born while the family lived in Shankill.

Chapter 2

Federation of Irish Manufacturers, 1944–9

In 1944 Erskine Childers, later President of Ireland, but then TD for the constituency of Longford–Westmeath, was appointed as a Parliamentary Secretary to the Government. This necessitated him resigning from his position as Secretary of the Federation of Irish Manufacturers (FIM). Kevin, aged twenty nine, applied for the position. It was to be the last job for which he would ever need to apply.

Eight applicants were selected to be interviewed for the position. At a meeting of the Council of the FIM held on 28 April 1944, Kevin was 'elected' after two counts, but only when the Chairman of the meeting, F.M. Summerfield, exercised a casting vote in his favour, the number of votes in favour of Kevin and the remaining candidate having been equal.[16] Kevin was appointed on a salary of £600 per annum, to rise to £700 after two years, and he began in his new position on 1 June 1944. His appointment was warmly welcomed, one commentator remarking that:

> If directness is the quality of the Northman, there is something of the quality in Kerrymen, who have been coming to the fore in business in recent years, especially in

Dublin, and now the Secretary of the Federation of Irish Manufacturers is a native of Tralee, Co. Kerry.[17]

Citing Kevin's Fellowship of the Chartered Institute of Secretaries and his membership of the London Association of Accountants, the writer observed that in his time in Dublin Kevin had 'built up a wide circle of friends who know that under his Kerry calm there is an all-round efficiency which is not merely a matter of diplomas'.[18]

While a Federation of Irish Industries had existed during part of the 1920s, Irish manufacturers did not have a dedicated representative body until 1932; until then, business-owners relied on the Dublin Industrial Development Association (DIDA) and its successor, the National Agricultural and Industrial Development Association (NAIDA). In November 1932, shortly after the election of a Fianna Fáil government committed to protectionism, a new Federation of Irish Industries (FII) was formed to represent the interests of manufacturers exclusively. Membership was confined to Irish nationals, so that 'Irishmen alone will have the government, ruling and guiding of the Federation in its work for the welfare and development of home industry'.[19]

In 1938 the Federation changed its name to the Federation of Irish Manufacturers as a result of its merger with the NAIDA. Membership was restricted to Irish citizens or firms where 'legal and financial control of the business is bona fide in the hands of persons who are citizens of Ireland'.[20]

The Federation unapologetically stood for the protection and advancement of Irish-owned and controlled industry. Its principal objectives were 'to unite the different manufacturing interests into one Federation where their views can be gathered together for presentation in whatever direction is considered advisable for the advancement of Irish Industry ... to secure that as far as possible, consistent with the National requirements, industrial development shall be retained in the hands of Irish Nationals ... to demand differentiation in the Assessment of Income Tax in favour of capital invested by Irish Nationals in Irish Industries.'[21] Speaking at the Eleventh Annual General Meeting of the Federation in February 1945, its President bluntly asserted that 'This Federation of Irish Manufacturers stands for the utmost development of industrial activity in this country, under the control of Irishmen, and in the interests of Irish people.'[22]

Throughout the 1930s the Federation pursued a relentless campaign in favour of economic nationalism, not just to ensure that national industries remained in national hands but 'for the protection and promotion of every phase of our national culture in opposition to its foreign counterpart'. The *Monthly Review* of January 1935 exhorted readers to:

> ... keep a strict eye for the future on your cigarette case: see that it is always replenished with goods which are the product of a nationally-owned factory. There is far too much laxity in matters of this kind, and they definitely reflect on the sincerity of our members.[23]

The protectionist creed of the Federation was echoed by Government industrial policy. The Cumann na nGaedheal government had introduced a series of tariffs on various goods during the 1920s in an effort to protect indigenous industries that were viewed as vulnerable. In 1926 a formal Tariff Commission was established. The failure of the Commission to deal with applications for the imposition of tariffs on a timely basis led to it being severely criticised by manufacturers. The coming into power of Fianna Fáil in 1932, on an overtly protectionist platform, saw a sharp rise in the range of goods that were the subject of tariffs, so that by 1936 nearly 2,000 tariffs were in operation.

The new Taoiseach, Éamon de Valera, appointed Seán Lemass as Minister for Industry and Commerce. This was the time of the Economic War (1933–8) between Ireland and Britain, caused by the former suspending payment of land annuities payable under a nineteenth-century arrangement and the latter retaliating with tariffs on Irish exports. In addition to overseeing a rapid increase in the number of tariffs, Lemass introduced the Control of Manufacturers Act 1932, the stated purpose of which was 'to permit outside control of industries only when the possibility of developing the industries concerned under home control had been exhausted'.[24] The hope was that, once protected by a wall of tariffs and by severe restrictions on non-Irish-ownership of business, local industries would thrive and create employment, thus reducing Ireland's undue and hazardous reliance on agricultural exports and providing a counterbalance to industrial imports.

The 1932 Act required companies not having majority Irish shareholding to obtain a licence from the Department of Industry and Commerce in order to operate. The Department, if inclined to grant a licence, was free to impose restrictions relating to matters such as size, location, labour force and output. Following intense lobbying from the Federation, among others, the position was further tightened in the Control of Manufacturers Act 1934, which stipulated that no more than 50 per cent of the issued share capital of an Irish manufacturing company could be held by non-nationals, that at least two-thirds of the voting shares were to be beneficially owned by Irish nationals and that a majority of the directors had to be Irish, if the licensing requirement were to be avoided.

The legislation proved fertile ground for lawyers and accountants retained by foreign industrialists to find ways of avoiding the licensing regime by creating artificial share structures for companies, so that those companies complied with the Acts and yet left a majority of control and profits in foreign hands. The principal architect of these schemes was the Dublin solicitor Arthur Cox, who would later play a central role in Kevin's business career and who was so adept at finding ways to circumvent the Acts as to cause one commentator to remark drily that he could 'put the Acts to music, if he was inclined to'.[25]

The Federation, which was a vocal supporter of the Control of Manufacturers Acts, continued to lobby Lemass and his Department throughout the 1930s and early 1940s to close the 'loopholes for those who wish to evade the spirit which brought them into existence'.[26] In reality, by 1944, when Kevin joined the Federation, the Government and Lemass, in particular, were starting to question whether the protectionist policies of the 1930s might need to be revisited. Speaking to the Federation just a few months before Kevin became its Secretary, Lemass expressed concern that protectionism may have fuelled inefficiency and warned that 'we must have ways of eliminating inefficient units and the intention to apply them ruthlessly when the need arises if the whole programme of industrial development is to be carried through'.[27]

The shift in Lemass' thinking from arch-protectionist was influenced, to a considerable extent, by his experience at the Department of Supplies during the Second World War. While the war had served to harden nationalistic isolationism—a fact from which Fianna Fáil benefited in the May 1944 General Election, in which it won an overall majority—it also had served to delay a potential crisis for the Irish economy. The ending of the war in 1945 brought into sharp focus the urgent need for

Irish industry to increase exports. This, in turn, persuaded Lemass that not only did protectionism need to be revisited but also that the sacred tenet of Irish ownership of industry might need to be diluted as well. In his *Memorandum on Full Economic Policy*, Lemass argued that:

> While it is desirable that all industries should be owned and controlled by Irish nationals, there is less reason for insistence on national ownership of export industries than of industries supplying only the home market and the employment of alien technicians will require to be facilitated.[28]

The Federation, which Kevin joined in 1944, was therefore in a state of some anxiety. The old certainty, i.e. that Government industrial policy would broadly mirror the Federation's own view of the world, was no more. Lemass' apparent change of heart, coupled with the impact on the Federation's members of the war in Europe and consequent concerns in relation to possible changes to the 1938 Anglo-Irish Trade Agreement—an Agreement that, in its original form, had not found much favour with the Federation—were the key challenges facing the Federation in June 1944. At that time, the Federation had just under 750 members, including 450 in Dublin and 70 in Cork.

A central part of Kevin's role as Secretary was the continuous lobbying of the Department of Industry and Commerce, a role that brought him into regular direct contact with Lemass. Reflecting on those meetings many years later, he described Lemass as:

> … an awesome, almost forbidding person. I never saw a man who could remain perfectly immobile throughout a meeting. He looked at you opaquely, and the only

movement was as he would fix his eyes on different speakers. He was ... a pipe smoker, but the pipe would lie there untouched. At the end of a meeting you would always know what Lemass's decision was going to be...[29]

A number of texts have referred to the relationship between Kevin and Lemass as being particularly close, one going so far as to assert that as early as 1947, Kevin 'at that time [was] perceived to be Lemass's stalking horse'[30] and that he echoed Lemass' view, expressed at the Federation's Annual Dinner that year, that 'Post-war problems must not be approached with a pre-war mentality ... protective tariffs and other import restrictions are going to be much less important to our industrial expansion in the future than in the past.'[31] Given that at that time Kevin was Secretary of an organisation whose fundamental creed remained unequivocally protectionist, the suggestion that he shared Lemass' views, never mind the notion of him as a 'stalking horse' for Lemass, is hardly credible. Indeed, it is an assertion that Kevin directly refuted some years later, pointing out that he did not know Lemass then and that he remained a believer in protectionism into the 1950s.[32] What is true is that over the years Lemass developed a high regard for Kevin's business skills, an opinion that would prove of considerable assistance later on when Kevin, as Director General of RTÉ, frequently found the television station in conflict with the views of government, by then led by Lemass.

His role as Secretary of the Federation required Kevin to make public speeches explaining, promoting and quite often defending the Federation's view of economic life. Over the years Kevin proved an effective and accomplished public speaker, understanding the need to lighten serious topics with the occasional well-timed quip. He was meticulous in his preparation, producing a number of manuscript drafts of each speech, with Peggy, who had trained as a shorthand typist, frequently taking on the task of typing the final version for him. He insisted on arriving early at the venue where he was to deliver a speech to check the microphone and the layout of the room. He had a keen eye towards what might attract media interest and, from an early stage, was adept at attracting headlines in the next day's papers.

One of Kevin's first significant public speaking appearances was at the Dublin Rotary Club in February 1945, where he delivered a paper entitled, 'Thoughts on Irish Industry'. In that paper, which was widely quoted in the media, he argued that the intensity of industrial development in Ireland in recent years 'had possibly obscured the fact that we have in this country an industrial history nearly as lengthy and as stormy as that of our politics'. He proceeded to take his listeners on a guided tour of Irish industrial history, from pre-Norman times, when Ireland conducted 'a thriving export and import trade with Continental countries', through the arrival of the Normans and the subsequent 'boom period', on to the sixteenth century when Galway was 'one of the greatest ports of the British Islands', through the growth of such diverse industries as glass manufacturing, glove-making and brewing, then the disaster of the Famine and the rebirth of industry in the newly independent State, which, Kevin suggested, should not be seen as a 'novelty' but rather as 'a recovery of a position which is our birthright as great in extent as any other attainment or characteristic of Irish Life'. The opportunity was not missed to underline the need for continued protectionism, on which policy, he declared, 'depends our economic independence – without which our political freedom becomes an empty formula'.[33]

When Kevin was invited to address the Rotary Club again in November 1946, his paper was much sterner in tone and even more strident in its defence of protectionism and the other preoccupations of the Federation. In praising the 'great strides' in industry over the previous twenty-five years, he questioned whether agriculture, the 'greatest industry in this country', had made similar progress. He observed that Denmark, 'a country of conditions, size, and population very comparable to ours, had reached an unassailable position in the World as a producer of agricultural goods, while in no way neglecting the development of its other industries.' He wondered whether, in the context of a more vibrant agriculture industry, 'our top-heavy capital city [would] continue to attract to its ever-swelling population our young men and women whose natural environment is the farm; would we still have need to send abroad those who by-pass the city, or, having arrived, found that its glamour could not fill an empty stomach.'[34]

Kevin then turned to the question of protection for industry and tariffs, which he advocated 'without apology'. It was critical, he argued, that the energies of Irish producers 'be not dissipated by the great productive organisations of other countries, whose interest would not be the economic advancement of this country, but solely the development of their export trade or even disposal of their surplus production at prices by which our relatively small units of production would be far out-classed.' He concluded with a blunt challenge to the critics of protectionism:

> To those unversed critics sitting high on the ditch of their complacency I say, get down on one side or the other and get on with the job. If they can function on our side in their occupations as well as they advocate policies for those in

others, they will contribute materially to the aspiration of all of us – our continued and greater prosperity as a nation.[35]

In early 1938 officials from Ireland and Britain had begun negotiations on a trade agreement aimed at bringing the Economic War to an end. The need to find an eager market for Irish agricultural produce meant, of necessity, that some elements of the protection afforded to Irish manufacturers would have to be sacrificed. The Anglo-Irish Trade Agreement was signed on 25 April 1938. It was to apply for a three-year period and continue thereafter subject to six months' notice of termination. A number of its provisions were viewed with a mixture of suspicion and hostility by the Federation, but the outbreak of war in September 1939 suspended the impact of the new arrangements. When the war ended six years later, the Federation renewed its campaign to ensure that its concerns would be taken into account by the Irish Government in any renegotiation of the Agreement.

Speaking at the Federation's AGM in February 1947, its President, P.L. McEvoy, argued that the 1938 Agreement had been overshadowed by two other agreements signed on the same day: 'The handing back of the Treaty Ports to this country and the wiping out by a payment of £10 million of the Land Annuities were outstanding victories for the Irish Government. The provisions of the Trade Agreement which we consider inimical to Irish industrial development were victories for the other side.'[36] As one commentator put it, the 1938 Agreement again demonstrated the subordination of economic objectives to nationalistic aspirations.

By 1948 it was clear that the Government was intent on revising the terms of the Agreement. If anything, the creation of an Inter-Party Government in February of that year, led by John A. Costello, which brought to an end sixteen years of Fianna Fáil rule, was likely to hasten that review. The Federation was equally determined that on this occasion its concerns would be taken into account.

The Federation's new President, P.J. Kavanagh, wrote to Costello in April of that year in the following terms:

> My Council requires me to convey to you and to your Government its most urgent concern with impending trade negotiations with Great Britain in the immediate future.
>
> In the considered opinion of my Council, the assured future of Irish Industry as a part of our national economy may well turn upon the anticipated revision of the 1938 Trade Agreement. For this reason it is asked of you with a full consciousness of the gravity of the situation that the Government Delegation would equip itself with all the resources available to it in the form of prior consultation with this Federation on the salient features of our industrial policy vis-à-vis Great Britain.
>
> Equally, and to ensure that the significance of the trade negotiations day by day be appreciated in all of their likely efforts, my Council asks that you would request of it to send to London a chosen and experienced deputation to be available on the spot for consultation by the Government's Delegation as necessity would arise.
>
> With my Officers, I shall be at yours and your Ministers' disposal at any time to consider these proposals.[37]

When the Government declined to issue an invitation to the Federation to play a direct role in the proposed renegotiation of the Trade Agreement, Kevin and the Federation's Council decided to go on the offensive. A Special General Meeting of the members of the Federation was convened at the Gresham Hotel in Dublin on 11 May 1948. In advance of the meeting, Kevin circulated to all members a detailed memorandum on the subject, which included the full text of each of the nineteen Articles of the 1938 Agreement, with an explanatory note on each Article.

It was clear that the hostility the Federation had expressed towards the Agreement when it was signed in 1938 had not diminished in the intervening decade. The tone of the memorandum was set by Kevin's commentary on Article 1 of the Agreement, which had provided for the entry into Great Britain, 'free of Customs Duty', of certain Irish goods:

> The experience of Irish manufacturers in recent years is, of course, that although Britain has had free and uncontrolled entry into our market, she has conceded no reciprocal facilities. If Britain's refusal to accept our goods is based on interpretation to their advantage of the above Article, our interpretation must be that it could never have been agreed –by implication or otherwise–that we would give away our capacity to compete in the British market. In present conditions when a fruitful opportunity is given to Irish manufacturers to establish themselves in the British market, it is vital that it is clearly established that so long as Britain has the right of entry for her goods into this country, irrespective of the conditions of entry, an equal right must be conceded by her to our manufacturers.
>
> It is too well known now to Irish manufacturers that measures of protection adequate in one set of circumstances can be rendered all to be ineffective by the changing policies of other countries, and the provision of this Article whereby greater protection than that obtaining

in April, 1938 may not be given to industries in this country is a hazard that the industrialist cannot ignore.

By implication ... products in the Schedule not manufactured in this country in 1938 never could enjoy any measure of protection in the quite likely event of their already, since, or in the future, being produced here by the establishment of an Irish enterprise. More clearly expressed, a definite restriction is placed on the establishment in this country of new industries enumerated in the Schedule referred to in so far that, irrespective of the handicaps of inception and growth, they cannot be given any measure of protection.[38]

His views on Article 5 of the Agreement, whereby the Irish Government had undertaken to admit certain British products 'free of Customs Duty and quantative regulation', were even more strident:

This is the first of several covenants inimical to the interests of industrial activity in Ireland. In effect, this section prevents the Irish Government-so long as the Agreement remains in force-EVER from giving protection by tariff or quota to the long list of manufacturers enumerated in Schedule 2, Part 1.[39]

In commenting on Article 8 of the Agreement, Kevin came to the core of the issue when he observed that:

The pit-falls for Irish industry in this Article are the difficulty of reconciling the continuance of 'adequate protection' for our industries with the granting of 'full opportunity of reasonable competition' to British manufacturers.[40]

The members of the Federation represented at the meeting in the Gresham Hotel left Kevin and the Federation's Council in no doubt that they viewed the proposed renegotiation of the 1938 Agreement as being of critical importance. The Chairman of the Cork Regional Group argued that unless the negotiating team comprised representatives of both industry and Government, he saw little future for Irish industry, either for internal or export trade.[41] He went further by citing an example of an agreement between Denmark and Great Britain, where the Danish negotiating body had been led by trade representatives while the Government negotiators had been in a relatively secondary capacity.[42]

There was a widely held view at the meeting that Ireland was in a much stronger bargaining position than in 1938 and therefore that the 'dictatorial' nature of the original agreement could now be reversed. Inevitably there was a concern, as expressed by Mr Folwell of Connolly Shoes Limited, Dundalk, among others, that 'the attitude of the Government in relation to trade agreements appeared to be the procurement of an advantage for agriculture at any cost and generally at the cost of industrial welfare'.[43]

As the meeting progressed, attitudes hardened with regard to how Britain had behaved both in the 1938 negotiations and in the intervening decade. 'England protected herself against Ireland,' proclaimed Senator F.M. Summerfield, 'and there could be no crime in Ireland doing likewise in respect of her industries.' He continued, 'The negotiating advantage today lay on our side and we must demand the right of entry to the British market on similar terms as those enjoyed by British manufacturers entering this market together with the untrammelled right to protect ourselves as we would see fit.'[44] At the end of the meeting a motion was carried unanimously to the effect that 'in view of the parlous condition of many Irish industries, the meeting demands of the Minister for Industry & Commerce that he immediately take every step within his power to protect its crumbling fabric.'[45]

The negotiations between representatives of the Irish and British Governments began on 17 June 1948 in London. The Irish delegation comprised the Taoiseach John A. Costello, the Tánaiste and Minister for Social Welfare William Norton, the Minister for External Affairs Seán MacBride, the Minister for Agriculture James Dillon, the Minister for Finance Patrick McGilligan, the Minister for Industry and Commerce Daniel Morrissey and the Irish High Commissioner Mr J. Dulanty. The British Government fielded an equally high-powered team, including Prime Minister Clement Attlee and the Chancellor of the Exchequer Stafford Cripps.

While the Federation was not directly involved in the negotiations, through Kevin's persistence it nonetheless achieved a central role. Kevin and Mr P.J. Kavanagh, President of the Federation, were asked by the Government to make themselves available, in London, for consultation. They travelled to London on 17 June and stayed there throughout the negotiations. They met with the Minister for Industry and Commerce or his representatives two or three times each day and were kept informed, in confidence, on the progress of the talks. During their stay the only member of the Irish delegation who did not meet with them was James Dillon, the Minister for Agriculture. Dillon caused quite a stir in London, with one newspaper reporting that 'his colourful expletives and extravagant gestures have been seized upon with delight by the columnists and political commentators in the more popular papers'. Among Dillon's more dramatic contributions was a threat that Ireland might 'drown Britain in eggs'.[46]

Each member of the Irish delegation was armed with a brief summarising the Federation's concerns in relation to the Agreement. The *Irish Press* reported that the brief, which was prepared by Kevin, contained a clear statement of the requirement for Ireland to have an equal right for entry of goods into Britain as Britain had for entry of goods into Ireland. The newspaper reported that 'although there is nothing in the official statement issued by the British Government ... to indicate it, it is naturally assumed that Mr. Costello opened this afternoon's conference with a recital of the policy which the statement enshrines'.[47]

A new Agreement was initialled on behalf of the two governments on 23 June 1948. Mr Kavanagh and Kevin attended the signing of the Agreement in the House of Commons. The Federation later made a guarded statement to the effect that the full significance of the Agreement was not readily apparent as 'the clauses dealing with matters industrial are far less clear than those defining what had been gained for agriculture'.[48] A former President of the Federation, P.L. McEvoy, caused some annoyance to the Council of the Federation by giving an interview in which he asserted that the advantages gained from the Agreement were negligible. The *Irish Press* described the new Agreement as an 'anticlimax', which, it claimed, 'repeats instead of replacing, the main provisions of the 1938 pact so bitterly attacked by Mr. Costello on the eve of the negotiations'.[49]

A meeting of the Council of the Federation was held on 30 June 1948, at which Kevin and the President reported to the Council on their involvement in London. At that meeting Kevin summarised his interpretation of the four gains contained in the Agreement as follows:

(a) The recovery of quantative restriction rights in relation to the free list, but subject to British concurrence.
(b) Capacity arbitrarily to impose tariffs on goods in the free list up to the value of 40%.
(c) An examination into the list of goods for which import facilities might be granted by Britain.
(d) The abolition of British right to nominate the priority of industries for investigation by the Prices Section.[50]

Overall, the Council believed that the renegotiation of the Agreement had achieved nearly as much as might have been sought. This view was not reflected in the media reports, however, with unnamed members of the Council cited as expressing 'grave disappointment'[51] with the outcome.

Kevin's tenure with the Federation also saw it embroiled in a bitter row with the NAIDA. Under the agreement merging the two bodies, the Federation agreed to take on the financial responsibility incurred in the running of the Permanent Exhibition of Irish manufacturers at St Stephen's Green in Dublin and further agreed to make good any loss incurred by the NAIDA, to a maximum of £300 per annum. It was agreed that the Federation could nominate sixteen of the thirty members of the Council of the NAIDA; the other fourteen were elected annually by the NAIDA. In fact, the Federation at no time sought to exercise that majority. When a dispute erupted between two factions in the NAIDA seeking control of the organisation, the Federation and its Council were joined as co-defendants in the ensuing litigation, which lasted a number of years. Several attempts were made to resolve the dispute, but according to the Federation's then President, P.L. McEvoy, in his address to the Federation's AGM in February 1947, these were 'met only with rebuffs, antagonism and breaches of plighted word'.[52] At one point, Kevin wrote a letter in strong terms to each of the national daily papers denouncing those in the NAIDA, challenging the Federation's involvement with that association as 'disruptionists'.[53] Ultimately, the High Court ruled that the NAIDA did not have the authority to enter into the agreement or to assign its property, thus forcing the Federation to sever all links with the organisation while still leaving it liable for some of the association's debts and the not insignificant costs of the proceedings.

Reflecting many years later on his time at the Federation, Kevin recalled it as a very small organisation 'living in a protectionist society, arising from the advent of the first Fianna Fáil Government. Seán Lemass was the strongest protagonist of industrial protection. He was also the first man to recognise when it was time to end it and that we should be thinking in terms of the EEC, or free trade.'[54] On the question of how effective he felt the Federation had been in representing the interests of business, Kevin replied:

> Oh, I would say it was very strong. It was dominated by very strong personalities. Seán Lemass always kept himself and the Government aloof from the Federation. We were frequently in conflict with Government—a conflict born usually of industry's impatience that the Government was not giving it as much security as it would like to have. We had a Liaison Officer from the Department of Industry & Commerce, St. John Connolly, who used to attend council meetings. On a few occasions I had to telephone him to ask him not to attend as he would be embarrassed by the discussions. There was very strong feeling against British manufacturers. It certainly was not popular to import British goods, for example, to wear British cloth or footwear.

One unfortunate member drew upon himself the wrath of the Council of the FIM by having his Christmas cards printed in England. I think our preoccupation in those days was with 'Sinn Féin', with holding on to what we had. We were reluctant to recognise that changes were coming. One of my efforts was to open a window into what I thought was a very closed shop. I went to visit my opposite number in the Confederation of British Industry, Sir Norman Kipping. Eventually a delegation from the FIM went to visit the CBI in Britain. I think some of them went at least morally with a gun in their hip pocket.[55]

Chapter 3

Industrial Development Authority, 1949–51

In February 1949 Daniel Morrissey, Minister for Industry and Commerce, announced the establishment of a new agency, to be known as the Industrial Development Authority (IDA). Its primary purpose would be to advise the Government on industrial policy. It was intended as a means of addressing, in a focussed manner, the chronic underdevelopment in Irish industry, which the new, post-war order in Europe threatened to expose. Credit for the idea is generally afforded to Alexis Fitzgerald, a Dublin solicitor who, as son-in-law of Taoiseach John A. Costello, was developing a significantly influential role in Fine Gael thinking.

The functions of the Authority would be:

(1) To initiate proposals and schemes for the creation and development of Irish industry.
(2) To survey possibilities of further industrial development.
(3) To advise on steps necessary and desirable for establishing new industries.
(4) To advise on steps necessary for the expansion and modernisation of existing industries.
(5) To investigate the effect of protective measures, with

special reference to employment, prices, quality of goods, wage-levels and conditions of employment.
(6) To examine, if and when required, any proposals submitted to the Authority by the Government relating to the imposition or revision of tariffs, quotas or other protective or developmental measures.
(7) To give advice and guidance to persons contemplating starting new industries or expanding existing industries.
(8) To advise on any other matter relating to industrial development referred to the Authority by the Government.[56]

The intention was that the Authority would comprise five full-time members. Welcoming the proposal, P.L. McEvoy, immediate past President of the Federation of Irish Manufacturers, expressed the hope that the five appointees would be 'practical men'. In his view: 'An ideal combination would be a manufacturer, a financial expert associated with insurance companies, banks and the Stock Exchange, a representative of Labour, a nominee of the engineering profession and a Government representative.'[57]

Morrissey used the occasion of the Federation's Annual General Meeting, on 15 February 1949, to expand upon the rationale for the new Authority. He told the meeting that the proposed new Authority was necessary if industrial development were to proceed on a 'sound and logical basis'.[58] Referring to the functions of the new body, he said that he regarded its role in investigating protective measures as by far the most important.

There was considerable speculation in relation to the likely identity of the members of the Authority. The names most commonly mentioned were: John O'Brien, secretary of the

Federated Union of Employers; J.P. Beddy, secretary of the Industrial Credit Company, which was the State-owned bank; Senator Luke Duffy, secretary of the Labour Party and a former organiser of a national trade union; Michael Murphy, Professor of Dairy Accounting and Dairy Economics at University College, Cork; and, at a later stage, Kevin McCourt. In fact, as early as 2 March, just two weeks after his speech at the Federation AGM, Morrissey met with Kevin and offered him a position on the Authority. Morrissey had come to know Kevin well during the negotiations on the revised Trade Agreement with Britain. He would also have been conscious of the desirability of choosing someone whose nomination would be welcomed by the Federation.

When the names were eventually announced, there were four rather than five members of the new Authority. As expected, J.P. Beddy was Chairman, with the other members being Kevin McCourt, Luke Duffy and J.J. Walsh. Walsh was a director of Eason & Son and his name had not been mentioned in any of the earlier speculation. The *Irish Press* reported that John O'Brien of the Federated Union of Employers had been offered a position on the new body, but had indicated that he could not accept it.[59] Of almost greater interest to the newspapers than the identities of the new members of the Authority was the fact that Dr Beddy, as Chairman, was to be paid £2,500 per annum, with each of the others receiving £2,000 per annum—the equivalent of a Government Minister's salary at the time. In Kevin's case, this represented a significant increase in income over that which he had enjoyed as FIM Secretary—'an undreamed of salary', as he later described it.[60]

The broad welcome given by the Federation and other business organisations was not echoed elsewhere. Fianna Fáil and, in particular, Lemass were furious at what they saw as an attempt to emasculate the power of the Department of Industry and Commerce. Predictably, the Department of Finance and the Department of Industry and Commerce were likewise unimpressed by the suggestion that a body would be established that would be responsible directly to the Minister, thereby by-passing the civil service. Morrissey's experienced Cabinet colleague, Patrick McGilligan, then Minister for Finance, was also sceptical of the proposal. He prepared a detailed, handwritten memorandum in which he recommended a much more restricted role for the new body than it was eventually given. As a starting-point, McGilligan recommended that the new body should be a 'Board' rather than an 'Authority' on the basis that it would be

> ... highly dangerous to invest the proposed Board with authority, other than in relation to matters previously submitted to and approved by Government. Looking ahead it might create, otherwise, a very dangerous machine for the exercise of corruption. It would seem wiser to approach the Board, as in the first place, as purely a fact finding and advisory authority to Government, with executive powers to carry out matters or schemes but only on prior reports approved by Government. 'Government' is used rather than 'Minister' in so far as cabinet is protection as against foolish or corrupt Minister.[61]

The memorandum envisaged that the Board 'would be there to supplement and assist but *not* to supplant private enterprise. Its function would be rather to sift the credentials of private enterprise in the public interest.'[62]

It is evident that McGilligan believed the best prospect of limiting the power and influence of the new body lay in persuading his Government colleagues that the members of the

Authority should be part-time rather than full-time. The prospect of a full-time executive working in parallel with, but not answerable to, the civil service clearly provoked significant concerns, as demonstrated by the force of the arguments and the bluntness of the language used by McGilligan in support of a part-time body:

> The Board will obviously have immense influence on business activities throughout the country and will be placed in position of exercising very critical powers in relation to investment and finance. It must only exercise these powers in a highly judicial and conscientious fashion. To act judiciously and conscientiously, in relation to very powerful interests whether in business or in Government, one must feel oneself financially independent. This is achieved with Judges by high salaries and life appointments. Obviously this method cannot be used with this Board – therefore, it is much more preferable that Board be part-time and members not dependent on membership for their existence and livelihood. They must be free men not open to corruption or undue influence by anyone. Fees paid to members must be such as to avoid any easy danger of corruption – in other words one cannot remove all temptations but steps must be taken to remove the more obvious.
>
> Board members might reasonably be expected to devote half their time to attendance at the Board's offices – in other words to devote say 3 solid hours per day to job. The rest of the day would in any case obviously be necessary for contemplation and thought on the very important problems involved, reading and studying papers at leisure etc. The members should have plenty of time to keep

themselves au fait with public opinion, technical progress etc. The Board members should not have to do detailed, executive work which should be done by full-time employees. Members would guide staff in lines of investigation and study their reports.

It would seem essential that the members of this Board be selected from men who have established positions in society in this country, the personnel *must* be such as to command the confidence and respect of the community and in particular the ordinary business or commercial community. The latter must feel from the start that they will get a fair crack of the whip and that the Board is not a gang of crackpot socialistic planners. It would seem very desirable that the members retain their present private occupations and continue to make their living from them. Their fees from the Board should be to them some jam or cake but by no means their bread and butter. The job they are to take on is really a trustee job – something over and above the earning of one's daily bread.

To be judicial in relation to private enterprise, one must be free from jealousy and envy – one is only free from these when one has reached a reasonable success in life and members should only be selected from the latter class.

The Board should not be envisaged as a Board of master mind planners – to direct and plan the industrial development of the country but rather as a Board of fact finders and advisors to the community and to the Government on the activities of private enterprise. They are there to search out possibilities of industrial development to collect facts and statistics and to bring them to the notice of entrepreneurs in some fair and suitable manner. It should definitely not be within their scope or function to themselves to run or plan industry or any branch thereof. They should be purely an Industrial Development Advisory Board and it might be as well to title them as such.[63]

While Kevin would no doubt have been amused had he known of the Minister for Finance's fear that he and his colleagues might be 'crackpot socialistic planners', McGilligan must have been perturbed at how comprehensively his views and concerns were ignored by his Cabinet colleagues when the Authority was established, with four full-time members. In a letter to Dr Beddy, which was copied to the three other members on the day of their formal appointment, Morrissey set out clearly the extent to which the Government was determined that the Authority would be an independent entity:

> The Industrial Development Authority of which you have been appointed Chairman is a permanent autonomous body which will operate within the terms of reference set out in the warrant of your appointment. The Authority as a collective body and its members as individuals, will be responsible only to me and through me to the Government.
>
> As the Authority will function as an organisation distinct from the Civil Service it will not be housed in a Government Department but in suitable premises for the provision and equipment of which arrangements are being made.
>
> The staff of the Authority will consist of Civil Service personnel who will be assigned to the Authority in accordance with such arrangements as, after consultation with you and your colleagues, seem to me to be best suited to your requirements. The Authority will, of course, receive the full co-operation of the various Departments of the government in the exercise of its functions.
>
> Legislation is being introduced immediately to give full

effect to the Government's intentions regarding the Authority and meanwhile the Government desires that the Authority should operate with the fullest measure of freedom within its terms of reference and, in particular, should not be subject to or work within any regulations or procedure which in the view of its members, would hamper the efficient discharge of their functions.

Should the members of the Authority experience any difficulty in so operating they may rely on my support in overcoming it.[64]

The IDA began its work from premises at 14 St Stephen's Green, Dublin, in late May 1949. Speaking after the first meeting of the Authority, the Minister emphasised the Government's desire for the further development of industry, the expansion of industries that lent themselves to expansion and the creation of new industries, particularly those that could utilise raw materials found within Ireland.

A further theme that the Minister unveiled at the launch of the Authority—one that would loom large in the subsequent Dáil debates on the legislation to formalise its creation—was decentralisation. He said that he was anxious 'to emphasise the Government's desire that, so far as possible, industry should be decentralised. In other words, I mean that the new Industrial Development Authority would be expected to bend their energies towards the initiation and development of industries in rural Ireland.'[65]

The decision by the Government to proceed with the establishment of the Authority in May 1949 without the required legislation even having been published was the subject of some considerable criticism. James Larkin, a Labour Party TD, asked why, three months after the initial announcement, there was still no sign of appropriate legislation.⁶⁶ Seán Lemass seized upon the failure to produce legislation to launch a further attack on the whole concept of the Authority. Speaking in the Dáil on 25 May, he described the new Authority as 'only an obstruction'. He continued:

> The Minister said just now that he is going to set up the authority in advance of legislation. For the life of me I cannot see what good that will do. The public know that the authority is going to be set up, and they know the members to be appointed to it, unless there has been any change since the announcement was made, but they do not know what its powers are going to be. It seems to me that that body functioning without defined powers and without the public having knowledge of its intended powers can achieve no results whatever. I want to be quite clear in expressing my opinion that it was a mistake to decide to set it up at all. I think that it will constitute merely a fifth wheel of the coach, a wheel with a permanent brake on it.⁶⁷

The legislation giving effect to the new Authority did not get its first reading for some time, after which it proceeded slowly through both Houses of the Oireachtas before finally being enacted in December 1950—almost two years after the Government first announced its intention to establish the IDA and seventeen months after the Authority commenced its work. The delay in introducing the legislation may be partly explained by the ambitious agenda the Fine Gael-led Government had set itself after sixteen years of Fianna Fáil rule. There may also have been a view that, given the open hostility to the concept displayed by Lemass and the equally negative attitude of the Departments of Finance and Industry and Commerce, not to mention the obvious scepticism of some members of the

Cabinet, it would be sensible to give the Authority some opportunity to prove its worth before the inevitable battles in the Dáil and Seanad commenced.

Four months after it commenced work, the Authority submitted an interim report to the Minister, dated 27 September 1949, copies of which were circulated to Cabinet.[68] The report focussed on the need to increase Ireland's export trade, of which 90 per cent was going to Great Britain and 'the Six Counties'. The members of the Authority had consulted with a number of contacts in the United States, including Mr John Hamill, an Irish–American businessman referred to them by the Taoiseach. Hamill proposed the establishment of corporations in Ireland and the United States to promote jointly a vigorous publicity campaign in relation to Irish products.

A contrary recommendation was received from a Mr Strauss of the Organisation for European Economic Co-operation (OEEC) who, according to the report, 'would deprecate over-dependence on the sentimental value in America of goods of Irish origin as the American market in his opinion primarily requires goods competitive in distinctiveness, quality and price.'[69]

A Czechoslovakian citizen living in Ireland outlined for the Authority the pre-war measures adopted in his country. These had involved the establishment of a privately operated export corporation, subvented by government in its initial stages, which brought raw materials abroad, booked orders, took credit and currency risk and marketed Czech goods abroad.[70]

The conclusion the Authority reached after its initial research was that a specialised export organisation should be established, preferably by the manufacturers themselves, to co-ordinate all of the elements necessary to develop a vibrant export trade. For such an organisation to succeed, the Authority expressed the view that a government subvention would be essential until such time as the organisation could become self-supporting on the basis of charges to exporters. In addition, to help overcome the 'lethargy and indifference'[71] of many manufacturers to export trade, the Authority suggested that financial inducements might be required in the form of tax remission on export profits, bonuses on currencies arising from exports and a guarantee against the risk of defaulting debtors. Kevin's former employer, the Federation of Irish Manufacturers, had separately been lobbying for some time for the establishment of a dedicated export body.

The circulation of its first interim report brought the Authority back into the firing line of the Department of Finance. A memorandum prepared for McGilligan clinically rejected each of the Authority's recommendations in turn. According to the memorandum, the best chance of increasing earnings or dollars was from '(a) the encouragement of the tourist traffic and (b) the revival of the sweepstakes'.[72] The Authority's proposal that the new export organisation should provide support services and information to exporters was already catered for by the Consular Service, while the proposal on financial inducements had previously been rejected by the Revenue Commissioners on the basis that taxation of profits 'does not lend itself to being used in endeavours to bring about particular economic results'.[73] The final paragraph of the memorandum showed the extent of the Department's hostility to an organisation only four months in operation:

> In general, it may be said that there is an air of unreality about this interim Report of the I.D.A. It does not seem to come to grips with the problem at all. If, however, the Government agree to the proposals, there is not the

slightest doubt that the manufacturers will receive the I.D.A. with open arms. Why shouldn't they? The State will then be doing for them something which they should do themselves.[74]

There is no record of any formal Government response to the Authority's interim report. A dedicated export organisation, Corás Tráchtála, was established in late 1951, but with much more limited functions than suggested by the Authority and against a very different policy backdrop.

The extent of the hostility of the civil service towards the new Authority is further illustrated by a memorandum sent to the Taoiseach by the Secretary of his Department following a meeting held between senior civil servants from a number of Departments, comprising the Foreign Trade Committee and the Authority members, on 11 November 1949. The principal topic for discussion was the Authority's interim report to the Government regarding the development of industrial exports. The Secretary told the Taoiseach:

> I was not satisfied at the manner in which this discussion was conducted. The Government decision of the 18th October, 1949, gave me, and indeed other members of the Foreign Trade Committee, the impression that consultation between the Committee and the Industrial Development Authority was intended by the Government. There was no real consultation today and I formed the impression that the members of the Authority was unwilling to discuss his [sic] proposals for the development of industrial exports at any length.
>
> The Chairman of the Industrial Development Authority did say that he would welcome information from members of the Committee concerning the operation in other countries of export institutions of the kind contemplated

in his own proposals. He did not, however, ask for the views of the Foreign Trade committee on his own proposals.

I feel that this attitude by the Industrial Development Authority to this particular problem is unsatisfactory.[75]

The core complaint of the civil servants who attended the meeting was a belief that the IDA was operating in parallel with the Departments without bothering to learn what work had already been done by the Departments on particular topics. The solution proposed to the Taoiseach was, in effect, that an instruction be given to the IDA to consult with Departments in advance of taking action:

> I suggest it would be well if, in future, before the Industrial Development Authority undertake an investigation on behalf of the Government they should be instructed to enquire from the Minister for Industry and Commerce whether any investigation of a somewhat similar kind has been undertaken in that Department or elsewhere in the public service and, if so, whether the Minister will place the results at the disposal of the Authority. It is no doubt advantageous that the Industrial Development Authority should in the ordinary course of its work be free from the procedural arrangements of normal departmental routine but where that routine has produced some experience which may be useful, I think it should be availed of by the Industrial Development Authority.[76]

It is worth noting in passing that the tone of the memorandum to the Taoiseach gave a very different flavour of the meeting from the minutes of the same meeting prepared by the Departments for approval by the Authority, which betray no sense of dissatisfaction.[77]

The outcome following the memorandum to the Taoiseach was far from what the civil servants had hoped. There was indeed to be an instruction delivered, but not to the IDA. A letter from the Secretary of the Department of the Taoiseach to his counterpart in Industry and Commerce recorded that:

> … the Taoiseach would be glad if your Minister would be good enough to make arrangements that will ensure that, as regards investigations being undertaken by the Authority of which your Department is aware, any on the subject matter of the investigations that is available in your Department and that might be of use to the Authority is provided at as early a stage of their investigations as possible.[78]

The only other record of work done by the Authority in its early days is a memorandum prepared by it for the Government in December 1949, which analysed a proposal by Seán MacBride, Minister for External Affairs, for the creation of a group of trade attachés that the Authority viewed as a 'valuable supplement' to the export body it recommended in its interim report.[79]

In truth, by late 1949 the focus of the Government was less on the day-to-day challenges faced by the IDA and more on the impending battle in the Houses of the Oireachtas to give it retrospective legislative legitimacy.

Much has been made of the virulent opposition of Seán Lemass to the establishment of the IDA. Whether his opposition 'revealed Lemass actually in retreat'[80] or was driven by the need 'to mend his fences himself with Fianna Fáil's allies in the industrial bourgeoisie following the industrial efficiency fiasco'[81] —a reference to his ill-fated Industrial Efficiency Bill—is open to debate. A more benign view is that he held a genuine concern that 'the ambiguous nature of the institutional arrangements between the IDA and Industry and Commerce ... weakened the integrity of the civil service'.[82] While this may have been true, it is difficult to avoid the conclusion that the driving force behind his opposition was pure party politics. After sixteen years in power, Lemass found it difficult to adapt to life on the opposition benches. One of his attacks on the IDA, to the effect that it was 'a typical product of the Fine Gael mind ... [of Fine Gael's] negative approach to national problems',[83] was resonant of his similarly partisan opposition in 1925 to the Cumann na nGaedhael initiative in relation to the Shannon Scheme, on the spurious grounds that it could be vulnerable to enemy attack in a future war. His subsequent attempt to justify his attitude towards the Shannon Scheme on the basis that he had been a very young man in 1925[84] could not be used to exonerate him in relation to his opposition to the IDA a quarter of a century later.

Whatever the cause of Lemass' conviction or irritation, the debates on the legislation witnessed many volatile exchanges. Since the Authority had already been in existence for a number of months, the legislation had the unusual feature that the four members were named in a Schedule to the Bill as being the first members of the Authority and who would continue in that position until 25 May 1954, when their initial five-year contracts expired.

In introducing the Second Stage of the Bill on 9 March 1950, Morrissey explained that one of the first tasks of the IDA would be to undertake a comprehensive survey of industrial resources, which, according to the Minister, was essential due to the lack of hard information:

> We do not know at present, for example, how much capital is invested in industry or how it is represented by buildings, by plant and machinery, by stocks of raw materials or of

> partly finished or finished goods, by debtors and by other assets. Neither do we know how these vary from year to year and from industry to industry. We do not know how industry is financed – e.g. the extent to which the capital is provided by shareholders, debenture holders, bankers, creditors and reserves. We do not know how many shareholders have provided the capital nor have we any information as to the dividends they receive, which is itself an indication of whether times are good or bad. Much more information can be obtained than is now available in respect of each principal industrial product, as to the extent and type of employment given, as to wages and earnings, labour turnover, welfare schemes, unemployment experience, etc.[85]

In response, Lemass returned to his horse-and-cart analogy:

> I suppose that a Government which can think of no other suggestion for the solution of national difficulties than the establishment of a commission is entitled to describe as 'more comprehensive approach' the proposal to set up an Industrial Development Authority. Supporters of popular racehorses frequently proclaim their merits by asserting their capacity to win dragging a cart. Irish industry is being asked now to show its merit by winning the race for increased productivity dragging a cart, a cart without wheels.[86]

He then went on to record his unequivocal objection to the whole principle of the Authority and, while emphasising that his opposition was not to the four named IDA members, stated his firm intention to abolish the body on Fianna Fáil's return to power:

I am opposed to the Bill in principle and, whatever views I may have about the individuals, I do not propose to express them. But, in fairness to them and to anyone else who may be now or who may in the future become associated with this Industrial Development Authority, I want them to understand that my opposition and the opposition of Deputies on this side of the House to the whole idea in this Bill is fundamental and that at the earliest possible occasion we will terminate it.

I do not want the individuals concerned to feel that, in taking action to terminate it, we are animated by an hostility to themselves as individuals. Our hostility is to this Bill and to the principle of it. It may be that the Minister will remain in office and that these people will continue to carry out his functions for him; but, if ever that situation ceases and the party on this side of the House becomes the Government, the functions of the Minister for Industry and Commerce will be resumed by whoever is nominated to that post and these subsidiary bodies will cease.[87]

Lemass' opening salvo was met in kind by a Government backbench TD who attacked Lemass' record as Minister and declared that 'many ugly monuments rear their heads in this country as gaunt evidence of his complete inefficiency'.[88] One of the strongest advocates for the Authority was T.F. O'Higgins, who dismissed the contribution of Lemass as that of a 'very petulant politician'[89] and went on to say that the Authority had 'considerable support both from employers and employees in Irish industry'.[90]

It is noteworthy that at no stage during the debates was reference made to the interim report the Government had received from the Authority. Lemass had posed the question at an early stage as to whether it was not 'reasonable to expect that the Minister, when introducing this Bill, would have produced one single achievement of this Industrial Development Authority?',[91] but throughout the debates Morrissey refused to give any detail, limiting himself to general statements that the Authority 'have had in ten months over two hundred and fifty industrial proposals, many of them, I grant you, small, some of them very small, some of them pretty big, a few of them very big'.[92]

While Lemass had been careful not to personalise the debate in respect of the four members of the Authority, it was evident that he took particular exception to the appointment of Luke Duffy, the Labour Party Senator. When, as the legislation came close to being enacted, a TD stated in a debate on 16 November 1950 that he had a 'shrewd suspicion' that Lemass had 'some kind of personal prejudice against some of the members of this Authority',[93] Lemass had declared that 'we could debate their mothers' people, because they are named in the Bill. We have shown a marvellous restraint'.[94] Later, when proposing an amendment that the term of office of the IDA members should expire in May 1953, rather than May 1954, so that a new Government elected after the anticipated 1953 General Election would be free to abolish the Authority, Lemass sarcastically stated that he realised that 'if there is a change of Government in 1953, the Labour Party will desire to recall to their service the very energetic officials whom they have so magnanimously lent to the public service'.[95] Lemass then declared that in his view the Government did not have the authority to agree terms with the four members of the Authority without the sanction of the Dáil, and that it was 'surely making a farce of the Dáil to suggest that, because the government eighteen months ago did something and came belatedly now to seek approval, we are bound to give our approval. Of course we are not'.[96]

As the debate neared its end, one TD asserted that Lemass, on the Second Reading of the Bill, had used the words 'pompous ass' to describe one member of the Authority.[97] Lemass failed to deny the charge and merely argued that the Official Reports of the Committee Stage had not been published, leading to the following exchange:

> **Mr Davin**: Is it not, unfortunately, on official record that, on the Second Reading, you described one of the members as an ass?
> **Mr Hickey**: And a pompous one at that.
> **Mr Lemass**: That is the Deputy's adjective.[98]

Given the continuing hostility of the key Government Departments, the tone of the Oireachtas debates and Lemass' open threat to abolish the Authority, it is unsurprising that morale was low among the members of the Authority. The eight-point mandate given to it on its establishment was as wide and challenging a brief as that of many full Departments, yet the Authority was expected to deliver with very limited resources. As one commentator put it, 'without executive power and finance, the IDA quickly become an overworked institution which could not develop policy'.[99]

A meeting was held on 20 October 1950 between the members of the Authority and members of the Government at which Dr Beddy 'expressed the considered view that unless adequate staff was made available to the Authority, and unless capital for the creation and development of industries were made more readily available, the Industrial Development Authority will be unable to fulfil the task allotted to it by the Government.'[100] Running through each of Beddy's proposals was a common thread of the need for the IDA to be given even greater autonomy. On the question of staff, he estimated that an additional twenty senior staff would be needed and that the Authority should have power to recruit staff directly and should not be limited to existing members of the civil service. On the provision of capital, he argued that the policy of the Department of Finance in considering applications for trade loans was too restrictive, that the capital of the Industrial Credit Corporation should be increased significantly and that the Authority should have the power to erect factories, which could then be leased to manufacturers.

The position adopted by the IDA received strong support from one Government Minister. In a memorandum prepared for the Government, Seán MacBride strongly supported the proposals made by Dr Beddy on the basis that 'the Government have entrusted the IDA with the responsibility for industrial development: we must be prepared to treat them as a responsible and prudent body'.[101]

A combination of continued antagonism at civil service level towards the Authority and increasing tension between the factions making up the Inter-Party Government led to MacBride's supportive memorandum not being circulated to the Cabinet. A note from the Secretary of the Taoiseach's Department to the Secretary at MacBride's Department bluntly recorded that MacBride's memorandum was 'not in order' for a number of reasons, including that it 'exceeds three foolscap pages but is not accompanied by a summary' and that 'the name of the Department of origin and the date were omitted'.[102]

The only substantive objection to MacBride's memorandum was that 'the sanction of the Minister for Finance does not appear to have been obtained.'[103] On this point, the inter-Departmental note recorded that 'the Private Secretary to the Minister for Finance said today that the Minister for Finance has instructed him *not* to seek the observations of his Department on the memo'.[104]

Lemass need not have been concerned that the Government refused to accept that the period of office of the members of the Authority be shortened to expire in 1953. The Inter-Party Government fell in May 1951, only months after the Industrial Development Act was finally enacted. Fianna Fáil returned to power, and Lemass to the Department of Industry and Commerce.

In a wide-ranging policy speech to the Dáil on 12 July 1951, Lemass declared his intentions regarding the future of the IDA. Despite his earlier commitments to abolish it, Lemass asserted that he had always recognised that there would be some advantage in having a body outside the civil service with powers and resources to promote the creation of new industries, which he defined as 'industries of a kind that do not exist now or are not likely to be brought into being by private initiative'.[105] The remainder of the Authority's brief, including fixing import quotas, adjusting tariffs, export and import licences and all other matters relating to existing industries, would revert to the Department.

By the time Lemass announced the proposed new role of the IDA, Kevin had resigned from the Authority. In informing the Dáil of the resignation, Lemass stated that Kevin 'had been pressing to be allowed to resign for some time'.[106] In keeping with his desire to reduce the role of the Authority, Lemass indicated that he would not replace Kevin with a full-time member but would appoint an officer of the Department on a part-time basis.

Kevin's decision to resign from the IDA was not taken lightly. He spoke fondly of his appointment by Morrissey and 'the sheer pleasure of being sought by someone to do a nationally important job'.[107] It was, he said, 'the biggest thrill of my life'.[108] He recalled with some pride the fact that John A. Costello had said to the members of the Authority: 'Gentlemen, I want you to understand that you have the authority, the capacity and the stature of High Court Judges.'[109] He had, however, become increasingly disillusioned by the lack of control that the members of the Authority had over its staff, who continued to view themselves as civil servants, and was also disappointed by the failure of the Inter-Party Government to react favourably to the requests made by the Authority at the meeting with members of the Government in October 1950. On a personal level, he felt 'desk-bound, not at full stretch'[110] and that in comparison to his role at the Federation of Irish Manufacturers, 'the action was not as fast'.[111] He also felt frustrated by the significant impediment to the realisation of the Authority's objective of encouraging foreign capital arising from the Control of Manufacturers legislation. As he stated years later in an interview:

> In those days, in truth there was very little to offer. I remember we went to Belgium to see a company. What could we tell them? That Ireland was beautiful, the labour force amenable, we were all Catholics and went to Mass every Sunday. There were no grants of course. And we finished off: by the way, you won't be able to control the company![112]

There is some irony to Kevin's complaints about the negative impact of the Control of Manufacturers legislation—these 'terrible Manufacturers Acts', as he once described them—given his previous role in the Federation, where he had lobbied intensively to have the same Acts made even more restrictive!

It is also clear that Lemass' vow to dismantle the IDA on his return to power contributed significantly to Kevin's decision to resign. As a married man with young children, the prospect of being out of a job was, to say the least, unappealing. Years later, when sitting beside Lemass at a dinner, Kevin bluntly raised the topic. 'You threatened me,' he told him, 'my wife, my children, my livelihood.' Lemass replied: 'My dear Mr McCourt, what we say in the Dáil has no bearing necessarily on real life.'[113]

That Kevin had nonetheless taken Lemass's threat seriously is evident from interviews he gave in later life on the subject, and also from the timing of his resignation. Six days after the 1951 General Election, Kevin received a letter from Arthur Cox, the solicitor he knew from his time at both the FIM and the IDA. The letter confirmed a meeting at Cox's office that weekend with an individual who Cox described only as 'my friend'.[114] The 'friend' in question was James Carroll, Chairman of the Dundalk-based tobacco company P.J. Carroll & Co., on whose board of directors Cox served. The position on offer to Kevin was that of Executive Director of the company. The discussions took place immediately and Kevin was in a position to offer his resignation from the IDA with effect from 30 June 1951.

Chapter 4

P.J. Carroll & Co., 1951–9, and Hunter Douglas, 1959–62

When Kevin joined P.J. Carroll's in 1951, it was a relatively small company in a highly competitive market. Though publicly quoted, approximately 65 per cent of the shares remained in the ownership of the Carroll family.

The business had been established in Dundalk in 1824 by Patrick James Carroll, the son of a prosperous farmer. By the 1850s its sales had grown tenfold and its products—ordinary roll, common roll, pigtail chewing and snuffs—were known throughout the whole of Ireland and, to a limited extent, in England. In the late 1880s the 'Mick McQuaid' brand was introduced, followed in 1905 by the first cigarettes produced by the company, 'Emerald Glen', titles which, in the words of James Plunkett, wore 'the halo of a forgotten culture'.[115] In 1919, with an eye on the increasingly important Scottish market, the emblematic 'Sweet Afton' brand was launched, a name chosen for its evocation of the works of Robert Burns. The success of the new brand made significant demands on the production facilities at Dundalk, so a second factory was opened in Liverpool.

The company became publicly quoted in the mid-1930s, when the four Carroll brothers, James, Walter, Vincent and Charles, were joined on the board by Arthur Cox, Henry Guinness, the Dublin merchant banker, and Joseph McKinley, the company secretary. The extent to which the company remained, in practical terms, a very traditional family company is eloquently witnessed by the fact that the Chairman of the company, James Marmian Carroll, who appointed Kevin in 1951, was only the third Chairman of the business in almost 130 years, following his father Vincent Stannus Carroll, and his grandfather, Patrick Joseph. James Carroll, who had joined the company in 1901, also served as Joint Managing Director with his brother, Walter. It was not only at Board level that the company remained a family enterprise. Throughout the factory, at all levels, could be found second, third and fourth generations of Dundalk families employed by Carroll's.

In the 1950s the business was facing significant challenges. Prices of tobacco products were closely controlled and excluding duty payable to the Exchequer, the price of cigarettes was lower than it had been in 1939 (until it was eventually revised in November 1951). In the intervening period the company's costs in terms of wages, fuel, power, packaging and transport had increased dramatically, while the price of tobacco leaf had almost trebled. As a result, the one-time widespread industry in Ireland had been reduced to just eleven factories and had the questionable distinction of being the State's largest indirect source of revenue, contributing over £17 million in duty to the Exchequer in 1951 and almost £22 million the following year. Speaking to the Rotary Club in Dublin on the topic 'Behind the Smoke Screen', Kevin pointed out that this contrasted with approximately £4.75 million duty raised by Government in 1939.[116]

The ever-increasing level of duty was not the only issue. Duty was payable before the tobacco could be released from bond, placing the tobacco manufacturer, as James Carroll said at the company's AGM in 1954, 'in an even less favourable position than that of being an unpaid tax-gatherer as he was obliged to provide the Duty, free of cost to the Government, out of his own working capital, capital which, in current circumstances, he has to obtain either from shareholders or from his bankers on which he must pay interest in one form or another.'[117]

The combination of these factors resulted in the company's net profits for the year to August 1951 being a mere £10,888, down from £67,000 in the previous year. Many years later, Don Carroll recalled:

> In 1952 there had been a very severe Budget. There was hardly any work in the factory—stocks had been sold to the retail trade before the Budget. The employees were all kept on, dusting the walls and cleaning the machines. The factory manager was incensed when Kevin McCourt came back with a big Far East order. Overtime was needed to fulfil it and the workers refused to do it.
>
> Carroll's was not going well. The product was bad. Shopkeepers would say, 'Sorry, we've only Afton' … In those days there was no protective wrapping, no silver foil inside the packet, no cellophane outside. There was just a cheap cardboard pack and if cigarettes were kept in the shop for any length of time, they absorbed moisture from the air. It was really necessary to get the product right and then go on from there.[118]

Kevin recognised that if these challenges were to be met successfully, it was essential that the company's sales be increased significantly in short order. In his first job as a manager of a business, he drew on separate experiences from his time at the FIM and with the IDA to propose a twin-track approach incorporating themes that would inform the remainder of his business life: a comprehensive marketing strategy to increase awareness of the company's brands in the domestic market coupled with an aggressive expansion into export markets.

Over the following years, Kevin became a leading advocate in Irish business of the importance of marketing and brand development, the need for proper management training, the necessity to move away from the isolationist protectionism of the past and the imperative of identifying and cultivating export markets. He became much sought after as a speaker at business conferences and as a contributor of newspaper articles and opinion pieces. He viewed all of these as important opportunities to raise the public profile of Carroll's.

During his time with the FIM, Kevin had come into contact with many traditional, long-established businesses that had focussed almost exclusively on improving their production processes to near perfection and ignored, to the point of their own extinction, how they would persuade consumers to buy their products. 'The consolidation phase in the industrial development of the nation is over,' Kevin declared in a paper entitled 'The High Cost of Not Advertising', delivered to the first National Advertising Conference in 1952, 'and industry now faces a future in which the techniques of selling and marketing have as great an importance as those of physical production and management.'[119]

It was understandable, he argued, that marketing had not been given much consideration by Irish businesses because the first decades since Independence had been consumed by 'uncovering our latest ambitions to engage ourselves in manufacturing'. He pointed out that in 1951, eight manufacturers in Britain had spent more than £200,000 each on press advertising, while forty-seven of the leading Irish manufacturing firms had spent only £240,000 between them in the same period, and limited advertising to the Irish national daily newspapers. By contrast, British businesses had products that were household names in Ireland thanks to ongoing advertising in the half million daily and two-and-a-half million Sunday newspapers, plus two million periodicals published in Britain but sold in Ireland.

While Kevin became one of the leading crusaders in Irish business for better marketing and branding, he struggled to persuade his colleagues on the board of P.J. Carroll's, James Carroll, in particular, of the merits of spending money on such modernist notions. When he proposed a market survey of public attitudes to and awareness of Carroll's brands, he initially met with considerable resistance. In this battle he found a most unlikely but formidable ally in his fellow board member, Arthur Cox. At one board meeting, Cox produced a scrap of paper on which he had noted the number and names of discarded cigarette packets he had found on his daily walks from his office at 42 St Stephen's Green to the Stephen's Green Club. To the horror of his fellow board members, he revealed the low percentage represented by Carroll's brands. So concerned was the board by the results of this non-scientific effort, that they instructed Kevin to proceed with a formal market survey, the results of which gave little further comfort to the company, but won Kevin the freedom to embark on a widespread marketing campaign.

On the question of protectionism, when speaking at a Social Study Conference in Dundalk,[120] Kevin declared that protection of industry was an essential feature of industrial existence. Drastic and redolent of dictatorship as it was, he believed that it was a necessary shot in the arm to their deflated industrial consciousness. He believed that Ireland must eschew any theories of free trade. It was no more than a theory. In fact, it had never been practised anywhere in the world.

With regard to the efforts of the Government to interest external manufacturers in Irish industries, he thought the country had badly missed an opportunity in the immediate post-war years when a number of medium- and large-sized US manufacturers set up in different parts of Great Britain and Europe to meet the demand of the markets there. While some saw danger to national prestige and ownership of industry by inviting external interests to establish industries here, Kevin did not agree with that view. Instead, he argued that worthwhile foreign industrial ventures should be brought in openly and with public licence, rather than be subjected to subterfuge and manoeuvrings of capital construction to conform outwardly, but not in fact, with the law requiring Irish financial control.

As a member of the Irish Management Institute, Kevin contributed to a report on 'Education Management'[121] prepared by a joint committee of the Universities, the Dublin Vocational Education Committee and 'big businesses'. He later recorded that:

> The report holds as a primary consideration that, without the requisite moral fibre, no amount of training and education will equip a man (and, presumably, a woman) to become and remain a successful leader. But given that, all that is understood by 'character' and possessing intuition, experience and intelligence, leadership and the capacity to guide can be attained - and more effectively attained - by education and training.
>
> Good management is not accidental in the complexities and competitions of modern industry, but rather the fruit of education allied to training on the same basis or

personal attributes such as integrity, intelligence and energy.[122]

Just as Kevin's time with the FIM had underlined for him the importance of marketing, his experiences with the IDA had highlighted that Ireland was a small, competitive market, with the tobacco industry further constrained by severe price control. It was evident to him that export markets would be critical to the success, indeed to the survival, of P.J. Carroll & Co. Speaking to the Chartered Institute of Secretaries in 1956, he said:

> Our industrial achievements in less than a generation have been truly phenomenal but optimism must be tempered by realism and there is a long road yet to be travelled. We are seeking the best of all worlds with no natural competitive advantages, and for that reason, our export ventures must be all the more intense, the better planned, the more competitive and the more persistent. We have the great advantage of being able to study the mistakes of industrial countries which got away to a flying start a hundred years ago, and there is probably now more advantage for us than there is disadvantage.[123]

Later, in an address to the Advertising Press Club,[124] he said it was evident that Ireland needed to develop its level of exports substantially if the country was to maintain its standards of living, which were in many respects among the highest in the world. Export was a state of mind—there must be the will, the interest and the confidence, as well as the courage and the intention, to set about giving people abroad what they wanted rather than helplessly and vainly trying to sell them goods that were simply surplus to the Irish market's requirements.

Kevin dealt with the three basic prerequisites in exporting:

good products, price flexibility and presentation. Together these pointed to the cardinal requirement of exporting: a first-hand study of the markets by those competent to undertake and analyse such a study. In terms of information regarding, and understanding of, what sells in any market and why it sells, in Kevin's view there was no substitute for personal visits and investigation. The transfer of goods from a manufacturer in Ireland to a consumer in France, Hong Kong or Australia was a link in the chain of human relations and in his experience nothing was so productive of business as good human relations. There can be no greater and more effective sharpening of our swords to meet the challenge of competition, he argued, than by trying to get into export markets right now, by discovering our weaknesses and our faults and by having the intelligence and ability to correct them to good purpose.

Kevin's public espousal of the importance of exports was recognised by the Government and in 1955 he was appointed to the board of Córas Tráchtála, the State-sponsored export body. In 1956 Kevin's growing status as an influential business leader was further recognised when he was a Government appointee to the Capital Investment Advisory Committee. The Committee had as its remit to advise the Government, having regard to the needs of the national economy, on 'the volume of public investment from time to time desirable, the general order of priority appropriate for the various investment projects, and the manner in which such projects should be financed.'[125]

In a paper he published in 1958, entitled 'The Urgency of Exports', Kevin focussed on the hard graft associated with developing successful export markets:

> He who thinks that export trade is merely a question of sending samples and price lists to names and addresses

picked from a Directory is wasting his time and money, for he will almost certainly not even have a reply. Export is people and places and climates and politics; it is travelling and reading and studying conditions, tastes and cultures, and it is the expenditure of effort and time and money.[126]

Kevin could speak with considerable authority on the effort required to open up export markets. In his time with P.J. Carroll's he made a number of lengthy business trips abroad, each planned with near military precision. The trips required a considerable personal commitment by Kevin as it meant leaving Peggy and his children behind in the lovely Victorian house on 16 acres that they had bought, just outside Dundalk, when Kevin joined Carroll's.

The first of these trips began in late 1953, lasted over three months and covered nearly 40,000 miles, travelling first to Bahrain, then to Pakistan, India, Australia, Singapore, Malaya, Thailand, Burma, Hong Kong, Aden, Khartoum and finally, home. Christmas was spent away from his family, in Sydney.

Kevin enjoyed not just the challenge of selling Irish cigarettes in markets with established domestic manufacturers but the different cultural experiences offered by each country. He wrote many letters home to family and friends describing those experiences. One letter was quoted in the 'Quid Nunc' column of *The Irish Times*:

> 'Here it is winter, and so only ninety in the shade' – trying to thaw myself after Saturday's arctic exposure at Lansdowne Road, I read this in a letter from Mr Kevin McCourt with the greenest of envy. The letter came from Khartoum, one of Kevin's stops of a tour of export markets which would bring him to India, Hong Kong, Singapore, Malaya, Thailand, China and Iraq before he sees Ireland again.

Of the Sudan he says: 'Politically only a year old, it has much in common with Ireland in many respects – even to the extent of having a primary concern with the removal of statues to heroes of the occupation, in particular, Gordon and Kitchener. The main problem is who on earth is to replace them.'[127]

In 1955 Kevin wrote a series of ten articles for the *Irish Independent,* under the pseudonym John Dancel (an anagram for 'Declan'), in which he described his epic journey, or the 'magic carpet odyssey', as the newspaper had it. The articles represented a fascinating insight into a world few in Ireland would ever witness. A few extracts show how observant and inquisitive a traveller he was. Of the wealth in Bahrain, he wrote:

> Bahrain is built on oil, it lives from oil. This is one's first impression, the all pervading smell of raw oil which is a constant reminder of the fabulous wealth which lies beneath its desert sands and explains, too, the extravagant evidence of Western luxuries in an otherwise primitive part of the world. Here are Sheiks – 'Shakes', they call them – with personal incomes of £50,000 a day some of them, and desert palaces, harems, fleets of modern Rolls-Royces, armed bodyguards, and with sovereign rights in their own territories.[128]

Of the poverty blighting Bombay:

> For all its magnificence, Bombay is grim and unpleasant in the sights to be seen along the roads and footpaths – the deformed beggars, the blind, the legless, and worse than all of these, the indescribable misshapen or diseased figure which you do not quite identify because you look away too fast to have taken it in and you only know that there is

something either missing from or horribly added to a human frame.[129]

Of the drinking in Sydney:

> But for all that is consumed in the most concentrated drinking session that I have ever seen or heard of, there is little or no evidence after 6 o'clock of the effects which might be expected. One salutes the drinking capacity of the Australian with respectful if not envious awe.[130]

Of a funeral in Singapore:

> Their funerals are noisy, colourful processions which are inconsistent with what we Westerners look upon as a solemn occasion; but the Chinese believes that his friends and relations last ride must be made with pomp, pageantry and noise or otherwise their souls will never rest in peace.[131]

Of being Irish in Burma:

> My reception was a cold one and was accompanied by the steely observation that I should have to take my place in the queue. Then the officer's eye fell on my green passport with its harp-imprinted cover. His curiosity was aroused; he had never seen an Irish passport before, nor it seemed an Irishman; he reminded me that the Burmese for a number of reasons – which afterwards I discovered were not at all over-complimentary – are known and like to be known as the Irish of the East.[132]

Of childhood in Hong Kong:

> In the streets one sees children of six and seven years of age, usually little girls, carrying strapped on their backs a young brother or sister whom they carry without any seeming

interference with their childlike play. But they do not seem to be children as we know them here, and their faces are those of adults with the consciousness imprinted on them already that life is hard. There is a pathetic competence and maternalism about the manner in which they adjust the baby on their backs when he falls asleep and slips sideways in the bundle which holds him in position.[133]

And of coming home:

> Then off again, flying to the West, while the fever of homecoming mounted after months of travelling; flying out of the heat and the sun and the strangeness of strange lands and strange customs and different food, flying into surroundings and environs where I would be home again.
>
> Journey's end was in sight and at last I could see the familiar and well-loved outline of Collinstown in a mantle of soft snow, a carpet incomparable to welcome me back.[134]

Kevin later explained the motivation behind his lengthy export trips:

> I found out where the British tobacco manufacturers sold their cigarettes. I packed my bags and set off with samples and went around the world. I found we could sell more cigarettes in a three months' trip around the world than we could sell in Ireland for one year. That gave us a great breathing space, it gave us business, it gave us cash flow, it gave us profitability.
>
> … I did it because there was nobody else to do it. There was no use in dashing around Ireland saying, 'Please will you buy Sweet Afton?'[135]

The opening up of export markets coupled with a substantial

increase in home demand saw the company's profits increase to over £100,000 in 1955. James Carroll continued to warn that profits were still 'grossly inadequate', representing a return of only 2.64 per cent of capital employed compared to a return of 6.6 per cent in 1939.[136] One of the markets visited by Kevin that proved particularly successful was Burma. In 1955 Myo Aung, Secretary of a Burmese import and export company, visited Carroll's in Dundalk and reported that since Kevin's trip the demand for Carroll's cigarettes in Burma had 'gone up in leaps and bounds'.[137]

In 1957 Kevin embarked on a 23,000 mile trip around the Far East, Middle East and, this time, Africa, including Sudan, Uganda and Kenya. On his return he expressed particular hopes for the market in Iraq.

In June 1958, after a number of years' preparation, the company launched Carroll's Number 1, a new brand of tipped cigarettes that in the coming decades would prove to be of central importance to the business. So successful was the launch that Carroll's quickly gained 60 per cent of the filter-tip market and decided to stop advertising their plain cigarettes in favour of the filtered brand. The new brand caused the Carroll's overall market share to jump from 9 per cent to 20 per cent. Terry O'Sullivan, who attended the launch of Carroll's Number 1, referred to Kevin in his column as being widely acknowledged as 'Carroll's Number 1', a reference that was not well received by James Carroll.

In 1959 Sir Norman Kipping, whose acquaintance Kevin had made while at the FIM and with whom he had stayed in touch in the intervening years, attended a dinner in the Dorchester Hotel in London. The person seated next to him, Henry Soonenberg, an East German refugee from the Second World War, by then based in Holland, confided that he had a problem. For three months he had been unsuccessful in seeking a managing director for his business, Hunter Douglas, someone who would have skills in marketing its products, negotiating with governments and who would be responsible for finance.

'You've described someone I know very well,' replied Kipping, 'but you have no chance of getting him.'[138]

A few days later, Soonenberg approached Kevin with an offer: a position with Hunter Douglas carrying a salary almost four times what he was earning at Carroll's.

Kevin would later speak warmly of his time at Carroll's, reflecting that during his tenure there he had learned the challenges of production—'why a cup is a cup and how it is made'.[139] While he 'enjoyed a tremendous amount of freedom'[140] and the Carroll family was 'generous and appreciative'[141] of his work, the reality remained that it was a family-dominated business. With Don Carroll, a nephew of James, whom Kevin had encouraged to join the business, making his presence felt, Kevin recognised that notwithstanding his enormous efforts on the export side and his increasing profile in Irish business circles, he had got as close to the top at Carroll's as he was going to go and would not be appointed Chief Executive, no matter how long he stayed. Contrary to what Sir Norman Kipping had assumed, the offer from Hunter Douglas came at just the right time. Kevin discussed the opportunity with Peggy and they decided, 'Yes, why not.'[142]

On 29 May 1959 Kevin's appointment as Co-Managing Director of Hunter Douglas, Holland, the European affiliate of a major US aluminium and plastics company, was announced. Kevin was also to sit on the International Policy Committee of the corporation in New York. 'I am not intimidated by the job,' Kevin declared, 'as it opens wider horizons.'[143]

In his Chairman's statement to the Annual General Meeting

of P.J. Carroll's in December 1959, James Carroll announced record profits of over £300,000 and noted Kevin's departure, stating that he had 'rendered valuable service'.[144] Kevin's contribution to Carroll's was acknowledged more warmly by those who had worked closely with him since his arrival and who had welcomed his open and friendly approach. One colleague wrote to Kevin on his retirement:

> The people who, fortunately or otherwise, work for this company, and none more than I, have good reason to remember the many kindnesses, the helping hand so readily offered, and the unusually pleasant way in which our accumulated worries were smoothed out by you. All of this experience was rather startling in its novelty, as no tidal wave of generosity had ever previously threatened to overwhelm us, and appreciation apparently was a word unknown to the cognoscenti in whose hands lie the destinies of a great industry.[145]

Kevin spent three-and-a-half years working with Hunter Douglas, initially in the group's headquarters in Rotterdam, although he and his family lived in The Hague. In early 1961 he moved to London. His family again moved with him, although by that time Pamela was attending a private boarding school, La Chassotte, in Switzerland, Germaine and Deirdre were at the International School in The Hague, while Declan boarded at Castleknock College in Dublin.

The marketing skills Kevin had developed at P.J. Carroll's were used to great effect on the international stage while at Hunter Douglas. His love of doing business in far-off places continued: 'I remember we sold an aluminium awning to a hotel in Durban. We did not check the intensity of the winds. The thing blew down one day. I can't tell you how fast I got out to Durban to put things right.'[146]

While Kevin always spoke with great enthusiasm of his experiences with Hunter Douglas, the position entailed significant personal sacrifices, not least being separated from his family for long stretches of time. A car would collect him at his house each morning at 6.45am and, on the occasions when he was not travelling around the world, he was rarely home before 8.00pm. 'It was a high-powered company,' he later recalled, 'I hardly had time to draw breath. One was always going from one place to the next—an aeroplane ticket in one hand and a telephone in the other. It changed my family's life completely, brought us into a new environment, gave us new horizons and concepts.'[147]

Chapter 5

RTÉ, 1963–8

Kevin's extensive travels on behalf of Hunter Douglas found him in Accra, on the Gold Coast, in late 1962 when he received an urgent telegram from Peggy referring to 'a very interesting Irish proposition'.[148] Peggy had received a call from Eamonn Andrews, then Chairman of the Radio Éireann Authority. Andrews followed up with a letter to Kevin in which he said that he had learned Kevin might be interested in returning to Ireland and if this were the case, he would like to discuss with him informally the shortly-to-be-vacant position of Director-General of Radio Éireann.[149] Andrews had been encouraged to make the approach by Seán Lemass, who was now Taoiseach. Kevin replied that the letter paid him 'an appreciable compliment'[150] and he immediately set about changing his travel schedule to meet up with Andrews in London. Discussions continued over a number of weeks. On 26 November 1962 Kevin confirmed, from Johannesburg, his agreement to join Radio Éireann as Director-General.[151]

During the 1950s a number of reports by a committee chaired by Leon O'Broin, secretary of the Department of Post and Telegraphs, had advocated the establishment of an Irish television service. Central to the argument was the stated imperative of protecting Irish morals from the increasing influence of British television, though this may well have been, as John Horgan put it, 'as much tactical as ideological'.[152] O'Broin was a strong advocate of the establishment of a public service television station modelled on the BBC. This did not find favour with the Department of Finance, which was concerned about the cost implications, or with Lemass as Tánaiste and Minister for Industry and Commerce, who favoured a commercially run service. Ultimately a Television Commission established by the Government reported in May 1959, but its recommendations lacked consensus and were largely ignored by the Government, which instead proceeded to enact the Broadcasting Act 1960. The Act established a new independent Radio Éireann Authority, to be appointed by the Government, which would have the task of managing both radio and a new television station that was to be established. In addition to Eamonn Andrews as Chairman, the first Authority included, among others, a number of academics, the General Secretary of the Irish Transport and General Workers Union (ITGWU) and Ernest Blythe, former Minister for Finance.

In November 1960 the new Authority appointed its first Director-General, Edward Roth, an American who had established broadcasting stations in Latin America. He was given a two-year contract. Lemass had urged the Authority to have the new television station up and running before the end of 1961. They cut it fine, but on New Year's Eve 1961, Telefís Éireann was inaugurated by Éamon de Valera, President of Ireland, with the rather gloomy expression of concern that television 'can lead through demoralisation to decadence and dissolution'.[153]

The position that Kevin accepted in November 1962, in place of Edward Roth, was one of the most high-profile jobs in Ireland. The written media had displayed an insatiable appetite for stories about the new station during its first year, and the appointment of a new Director-General served only to heighten this interest. The newspapers of late November 1962 were filled with profiles of Kevin's career to date. Some commentators sought to read into Kevin's appointment a subtle shift in thinking on the part of the Authority to the vexed question of the promotion of the Irish language on television: 'It would appear, at first sight, that the appointment indicates a more modern approach to the question of the Irish language on TV: Mr.McCourt has not had any background as a language enthusiast.'[154]

Another newspaper observed: 'Mr.McCourt takes over a television system that is having protracted teething troubles. His task will not be easy and it may be said he will have to redirect policies and take a critical look at the present structure. Time, for the moment, is on the side of the new man at Montrose, but the public is restive and he will have to work speedily to capture, and hold, a wide following.'[155]

Others gave him unsolicited advice about how to run Telefís Éireann, telling him that in the New Year of 1963 he ought to 'rub it out and start all over again'.[156] A letter-writer to one newspaper expressed the hope 'that Mr. McCourt will do something to lift the level of foreign drivel being given us on the Irish sound and vision programmes. Telefís Éireann, particularly news, has reached the level of the lowest common fertiliser.'[157]

An open letter to the new Director-General in another newspaper, before Kevin's appointment was confirmed, opened with the words: 'Dear Director-General, Greetings, Salutations, and the best of flipping luck. You're going to need it all' and closed with, 'But in any case, dear Director-General No. 2, whoever you may turn out to be, our best advice is to enjoy life now while you can. Things are going to be worrisome from the moment you slide into the Director-General's chair.'[158]

Kevin later became the subject of the satire of Myles na

Gopaleen. In the course of a piece complaining about mispronunciations on the 'electric wireless', he said of Kevin:

> I cannot blame this gentleman for his preposterous title (for titular elephantiasis is strictly a Feeny Fayl syndrome) but if he does not act, I will register my annoyance in a subtle, sinister way. I will pull strings to induce either one or other (or maybe both) of the universities to 'honour' him. Then he will find himself a blushing member of the tribe of bogus Doctors who infest the townland.[159]

The extent of media interest in Kevin's appointment was graphically brought home to him in early December 1962 when a visit to Dublin to see his parents was the subject of comment in each of the daily newspapers, accompanied by photographs taken of him and Peggy at Dublin Airport. The cancellation of a separate visit merited the headline, 'Fog delays T.E. Chief in London',[160] while the eventual return of the family to live in Dublin saw the publication of a photograph of the entire family arriving in the city under the headline, 'TE Chief's family arrives home'.[161] Kevin avoided any comment on his plans other than to declare to the *Sunday Review* that his new role was 'a man-sized job'.[162]

The same paper published an interview with Peggy—'the quiet woman behind the new head of TV'[163]—whom they described as 'tall, attractive and blonde'. Peggy told the newspaper that confirmation of Kevin's appointment had been received on their twenty-first wedding anniversary: 'it was a lovely coincidence, after 21 wonderful years'. She described Kevin as a quiet man of simple tastes, easy to live with, but with high standards in everything, an avid reader who loved jazz, classical music and painting. Asked to describe her husband's greatest attribute, Peggy said that he 'is most interested in people and in everything around him. He is constantly exploring new ideas and listening to viewpoints'. Inevitably, she was asked about Kevin's interest in the Irish language and replied diplomatically: 'his father was a great Irish enthusiast and he was born into a very Irish home. Kevin's Irish is probably a little rusty, but it is alright.'[164]

The suitability of Kevin for appointment as Director-General was queried in Dáil Éireann. Dr Noel Browne TD asked why, in view of the fact that the Minister had made the case for the possession of experience in television and entertainment generally in the cases of both Edward Roth and Eamonn Andrews, he had not insisted on the same qualifications on this occasion. The appointment won the support of Fine Gael, however, for whom Liam Cosgrove declared that Kevin's appointment was an 'excellent choice'.[165]

The approach from Eamonn Andrews had indeed come at a time when Kevin was thinking about returning to Ireland. The gruelling schedule of travel for Hunter Douglas was keeping him away from his family far too much. The decision to return home was not without difficulty, however. The financial package offered by the Authority was very considerably less than he was enjoying abroad. Indeed, it was less in total than had been paid to his predecessor, Edward Roth. Nevertheless Kevin felt that the drop in income was a price worth paying. 'Hunter Douglas was a very successful company and a very generous one,' he later said. 'I educated my children with the money I made in Holland … I neither have nor wanted a yacht or a race-horse or a second wife.' Quoting Oscar Wilde, he joked: 'I'm easily satisfied with the best of everything.'[166]

Kevin's contract was for five years, running from 1 January 1963, at an annual salary of £5,500. He was also to be provided with an unfurnished home that he would rent from the

Authority. In spite of this, for some time the Authority failed to do anything about the provision of a house to Kevin and his family in accordance with his contract. The Minutes of the Authority meeting of 11 July 1963 noted the difficulties in selling the house occupied by Roth and the decision to revert to an earlier plan to build a permanent residence for the Director-General on its own property. The Minutes recorded a number of advantages of this approach, including:

(1) The Director-General would be readily available for emergency consultations, so vital and peculiar to the business of television.
(2) A suitable residence would be available for entertaining visiting dignatories etc.
(3) It would be financially much more desirable than continuing indefinitely to meet the cost of maintaining the Director-General and his family in hotel accommodation as provided for in the contract.[167]

Nothing further was done about building a residence. In June 1964 the Authority bought a house in Greenfield Park, across the road from Montrose, for £14,500, which was to be rented to Kevin, subject to the approval of the Minister, at a rent of £500 per annum. Andrews reported to the Authority in July 1964 that he had spoken to the Minister, who had told Andrews that 'he would be receiving a letter which might appear unsympathetic but that he, the Minister, was still sympathetic'.[168] A letter rejecting the proposal was received from the Department. When Andrews sought to have the Minister honour his verbal commitment, he was bluntly informed that 'understandings arising from conversation did not prevail and that only [the Minister's] written decision or agreement was valid.'[169] The result was that the Authority sold the house in Greenfield Park at a loss.

Kevin was faced with a significant challenge immediately on taking up his new position. The National Union of Journalists (NUJ) was agitating for wage increases for its members. At Kevin's first meeting, on 10 January 1963, the Authority resolved that it would be 'highly undesirable that the Authority should risk sparking off a ninth round of wage increases'.[170] The Authority requested that Kevin deal directly with the Union, but gave him no real mandate to reach an agreement. When strike notice was served in late January, Kevin redoubled his efforts and by the end of February he had come up with a formula that included a referral of part of the dispute to the Labour Court.

The manner of Kevin's intervention won him significant respect from the NUJ negotiators. A booklet produced by the NUJ, entitled *Journalists on Strike,* recorded that Kevin had asked to meet the Union leader personally:

> Mr. McCourt was non-provocative and was most helpful to endeavour not only a strike [sic] but any continuation of the adverse atmosphere that had existed between management and the journalists over the past year. He expressed his willingness to set up agreed liaison machinery within the organisation and to investigate and, within the bounds of human possibility, to solve all areas of dissatisfaction. With the greatest openness of mind he would look at everything with the agreed machinery reporting direct to him. He regretted that he could not offer more money than the £1,370 already offered plus adjustments within the scale. He said his approach to these adjustments would be consonant with his desire to reach a settlement and have a happy office.[171]

On a lighter note, Kevin's first few weeks in RTÉ saw him receive a lot of correspondence from listeners and viewers, including a letter from a woman when he was only three weeks into the job which said: 'Dear Kevin McCourt, [so-and-so] is a friend of mine and a friend of yours and he said you were a great man and I was delighted when I heard you were coming back to Ireland to take over broadcasting. I don't see any changes in the programme since you came back. I think you should go back where you came from.'[172]

A few months prior to Kevin's arrival, the first Controller of Programmes of Telefís Éireann, Michael Barry, had given notice of his intention to resign. In March 1963 the Authority appointed Gunnar Rugheimer to the position. Rugheimer, a Swedish national, had worked for many years for the Canadian Broadcasting Corporation as a producer and later as a programme director before joining MCA in London, where he came to the notice of Eamonn Andrews. His appointment was strongly supported by Kevin, who immediately recognised the advantage of someone with an international perspective.

Rugheimer was given a three-year contract. He brought to the organisation a sense of professionalism. According to one description he was 'a strong man who enjoyed and was used to all the demands on stamina and nervous energy which the daily slog of television make. He required the same commitment from others and could be merciless when he regarded their performance as falling below standard.'[173]

From the outset the issue of Rugheimer as a 'foreigner' was a constant undercurrent. Conscious of the need to guard against this becoming a significant distraction, Kevin reported to the Authority in June 1963 that he intended to work closely with the new Controller of Programmes until Rugheimer was 'really secure in his mind that he had acquired a feel for Ireland and things Irish'.[174]

Kevin later would describe Rugheimer as a man with a 'big,

penetrating voice',[175] who was 'tough, strong and intellectual' and whose only 'weakness' was 'intolerance with sectional interests in Ireland, what he would have called "unimportant" interests like the hierarchy, politicians and the Irish language people, roughly in that order.'[176]

In time, Rugheimer's non-Irish background would become a major point of controversy and contribute to his departure and that of Eamonn Andrews, but in the meantime he and Kevin became a very effective team. Rugheimer's detailed understanding of and passion for broadcasting complemented Kevin's considerable business experience and acumen. They enjoyed the unqualified support of Andrews, and they and he quickly formed a dominant 'triumvirate'.[177]

The broadcasting highlight of Kevin's first year in the job was undoubtedly the coverage of the visit to Ireland of President John F. Kennedy in June 1963.

In late spring 1963 word came to RTÉ that President Kennedy would visit Berlin in June of that year and would stop in Ireland on his way back to the USA to visit his ancestral home in Dunganstown, County Wexford. The White House let it be known that it would like full television coverage of the visit. Telefís Éireann, then only eighteen months old, had one outside broadcast (OB) unit of four cameras and limited microwave radio-link facilities. Notwithstanding this, Kevin, with enthusiastic support from Rugheimer, believed it was imperative that full coverage of the visit be undertaken. Tom Hardiman, who was in charge of OB facilities at the time, was given the task of planning the coverage and hiring additional facilities from the BBC and the UK's commercial stations.

The Department of External Affairs was determined to keep the details of the visit very confidential, which was a source of frustration to Kevin, who made several attempts to persuade the

Secretary of the Department and the US Ambassador to Ireland of the need for Telefís Éireann to be given adequate advance notice of the plans. Eventually, Kevin got to meet the President's Press Officer, Pierre Salinger, who handed Kevin a copy of the itinerary marked 'Top Secret' and invited him to 'take whatever notes you want'.

In addition to live television coverage in Ireland, the UK and parts of mainland Europe, the US networks wanted live satellite coverage. Telstar, an experimental orbiting satellite capable of television transmission, had a limited period of some hours each day when it was visible in northern Europe and the east coast of the US simultaneously. Thus, the first live satellite television transmission from Europe to the US featured parts of President Kennedy's visit to Ireland.

The Telefís Éireann coverage of the visit received warm plaudits from broadcasters throughout Europe and the USA. After President Kennedy's assassination in November of that year, Kevin sent a recording of the film as a contribution to the Kennedy Library, receiving in return a very gracious letter from Mrs Jacqueline Kennedy.

As his first year in the job drew to a close, Kevin found himself defending Telefís Éireann against separate attacks from two of the young station's most consistent critics: the Government, in particular the man who had recommended him for the job, Taoiseach Seán Lemass, and the Catholic Church in the form of Kevin's teacher from Blackrock College days, now the Archbishop of Dublin, John Charles McQuaid.

Lemass was an avid consumer of Telefís Éireann's current affairs output and since the inception of the station had never been slow to voice his annoyance at even the most trivial perceived affront to Government policy. He found a more-than-willing ally in Padraig O hAnracháin, head of the Government

Information Bureau, who frequently took on the task of making the Taoiseach's displeasure known to Telefís Éireann. In a letter to Lemass in September 1962, O hAnracháin reported on a meeting with Edward Roth and Jack White, head of Public Affairs at Telefís Éireann, and declared that Roth had given him the impression that 'he [Roth] would gladly dispense with most - if not all - of the present interviewers on TE - male and female - if he could find better but this, so far, at any rate, he has failed to do.'[178] In the same letter O hAnracháin expressed his strong reservations about the performance of the Authority:

> In the time that has elapsed since T.E. went on the air last January I think one thing has emerged above all others viz; that the Authority has failed to lay down for itself any firm line of policy in regard to its principal role as the National Broadcasting Station. It seems to give the impression of merely living from day to day doing the best it can to meet difficulties and problems as they arise. There is, I feel, an obligation on the Authority to harmonise with broad National policy and to see to it that none of their programmes on Television or sound run contrary to it. Instead of appearing to realise this the Authority would almost give the impression, at times at any rate, that either they do not know what National policy is or cared even less.
>
> It seems to me that, for the R.E. Authority, the time to experiment and adapt is now drawing to a close and that there is an urgent need for some new thinking in the light of the Authority's efforts and the results obtained to date.
>
> The R.E. Authority has, in my opinion, an immense job still to do if it is to measure up to the role demanded of it in the Nation's life.[179]

Two days after Kevin's appointment a discussion on Telefís

Éireann on the topic of emigration caused Lemass to report to O hAnracháin that 'The general effect was to leave the impression "nobody cares a damn about emigration or the emigrants." It was thoroughly bad and depressing, and represented exactly the approach to serious national problems that Telefís Éireann should not adopt.'[180] He said he intended to raise the matter with the new Director-General.

The first significant conflict between Lemass and Telefís Éireann during Kevin's tenure arose in November 1963, when Lemass summoned Kevin to a meeting at which he complained about the manner in which an initiative of the Government, Turnover Tax, had been dealt with on an edition of 'Thursday Topic'. Lemass demanded that Telefís Éireann broadcast a programme promoting the counter-arguments; Kevin steadfastly refused to do so. Lemass then met with Eamonn Andrews, to whom he acknowledged that he [Lemass] had been 'tactically wrong'[181] in summoning Kevin, since it was the Authority that he, as Minister, should hold accountable.

Andrews subsequently reported to the Authority that Lemass believed the Authority had a function to sell the idea of Government and to inform the public constructively rather than to 'knock' legislation passed in the Oireachtas and the decisions of the Government.[182] At the same meeting Kevin sought clarification of the Authority's policy: did the Authority wish that issues of public interest, although politically contentious, should not be handled?[183] He also robustly rejected any suggestion that there was a question of irresponsibility on the part of the staff. Following Kevin's contribution, the Authority resolved that the staff of RTÉ 'should make programmes on matters of public interest and controversy, handling them with courage and vision and without feeling that they had to play safe by avoiding issues in any area on which there would be conflicting opinions.'[184]

The letter sent by Andrews to Lemass on the day following the meeting acknowledged that the programme on Turnover Tax had been imbalanced and apologised for the failure of the programme to detail the 'positive' aspects of the tax.[185] Whatever the diplomatic nature of the formal response to Lemass, Kevin had succeeded in defending the broadcasting independence of the station to both the Taoiseach and the Authority—a fact acknowledged by Lemass, who later said to Andrews, 'If he [Kevin] was to take instructions from every Tom, Dick and Harry, he'd go mad.'[186]

Some months earlier Kevin had incurred, not for the last time, the wrath of Lemass' colleague and son-in-law, Charles Haughey, then Minister for Justice. Haughey had proposed to Kevin that whenever he or his Department issued a prepared statement of special interest or importance, the statement should be reported verbatim or not at all. Kevin could not agree, arguing that lengthy verbatim statements in spoken form would be self-defeating if they failed to hold the attention of a viewing and listening audience. When Kevin's position was communicated to him, Haughey wrote to his Cabinet colleague, Michael Hilliard, in the strictest terms:

> I am afraid we are completely at cross-purposes. I was referring exclusively to a very definite, limited category, namely specially prepared statements of particular importance issued as such by Ministers or their Departments. I think it is an appalling state of affairs that the director-general is not prepared to give these the recognition to which they are entitled.[187]

In December, Kevin faced down a further early challenge to the journalistic independence of his staff, this time from the formidable Archbishop John Charles McQuaid. Alone among

Irish media organisations, RTÉ had sent staff to Rome to cover the Second Vatican Council, convened by Pope John XXIII. Part of the coverage included an interview in Dublin with theologian Fr Gregory Baum, a Canadian with progressive views on ecumenism. McQuaid wrote to Kevin to demand 'by whose authority Rev. Gregory Baum, who appeared on a Telefis Eireann programme, was invited to speak and did speak in this diocese on matters of faith and morals?'[188] An earlier draft of the letter had referred to Baum as 'stranger-priest' and the diocese as 'my' diocese.[189] Kevin was unmoved and replied sharply:

> Since Father Baum is a well known expert on the ecumenical movement and was attached to the Council, it was taken for granted that he was well qualified to comment on the proceedings there. The responsibility for using Dr. Baum's services, of course, rests with Radio Éireann but we would assume that, if he required ecclesiastical clearance to participate in a programme of the kind involved, this would be a matter between him and the ecclesiastical authorities.[190]

As events transpired, Kevin had a much more significant confrontation with McQuaid over another priest. The hierarchy had established the Catholic Television Interim Committee, which was tasked with devising concepts for religious programmes. Noting the model operated by the BBC, the Committee also sought to encourage RTÉ to employ a full-time religious adviser. On Kevin's appointment as Director-General, the Committee invited him to meet them, an invitation he accepted 'as a not too visible priority'.[191]

Archbishop Thomas Morris of Cashel informed Kevin that the Committee, supported by McQuaid, wished to appoint a priest to the staff of RTÉ. Morris was taken aback when Kevin replied that the appointment would be made by the Authority, on his recommendation.

Kevin invited the Committee to submit names for consideration by the Authority. The person favoured by the Committee was Fr Joseph Dunn, who worked on the *Radharc* series of programmes. The Committee produced a list of three names, with Fr Dunn named first, and assumed that he would be appointed. The third name on the list was that of a Dominican priest, Fr Romuald Dodd, the only one of the three who was not directly subject to the authority of the Archbishop of Dublin. Eamonn Andrews and Kevin saw the opportunity to thwart McQuaid's ambitions, while selecting someone from the Committee's own list of recommendations. They appointed Fr Dodd.

When he was informed of the decision, McQuaid was furious. He wrote to Kevin that he understood he had appointed 'a' Fr Romuald Dodd and that he felt it necessary to remind Kevin that as Archbishop of Dublin, he was the 'authority' with sole responsibility for the expression of Catholic teaching and liturgy in the Archdiocese.[192]

Kevin sent a placatory reply, but refused to concede his position. The issue was eventually settled and Fr Dodd went on to work in RTÉ for over twenty years, but the episode, as Kevin later wrote in a note to Fr Dunn, had a 'sad ending':

> Some time later, I was at a reception in the old Nunciature, saw John Charles across the room, moved my way towards him and, as he disengaged, saluted him 'Your Grace'. He turned to me, said not a word, and swept past me with almost a disdaining swoosh of his elegant robe.[193]

The recognition by Lemass, in relation to the Turnover Tax

issue, that Kevin could not be expected to keep everybody happy did not prevent the Taoiseach having a further attack of outrage at the failure of RTÉ to pay appropriate homage to Government policy just a few months later. In July 1964 the Government launched the Second Programme for Economic Expansion and RTÉ broadcast a programme discussing its merits. The morning after the broadcast Lemass sent a memorandum to the Secretary of his Department, in which he described the contribution of Professor J.B. Ruane on the programme as 'misleading, apart from being shallow and destructive'.[194] The function of the Authority, he declared: 'should be primarily to support the Programme rather than to facilitate criticism, and certainly criticism must not be allowed to go un-answered. If there is any resistance on the part of the Authority, let me know and I will deal with it.'[195]

Kevin was contacted by the Secretary and he defended the programme as having 'served its purposes'[196] and as being 'at least 90%' favourable to the Second Programme. As with the Turnover Tax incident, Kevin refused to contemplate a 'make good' programme on the basis that it would be 'injudicious' to attempt such a rebuttal exercise and, further, that 'if he [Lemass] were to call for it, it would be all over Radio Éireann and outside that Government pressure had been put on him [McCourt]'.[197]

In January 1964 Kevin announced plans for the establishment of a closed circuit television series aimed at schools and to be known as Telefís Scoile, which would concentrate initially on the direct teaching of subjects that lent themselves to visual presentation, such as physics and chemistry. While Kevin was quite prepared to see the series funded out of Telefís Éireann's own resources, the Department of Post and Telegraphs insisted that the Department of Education foot the bill.

In the same month Kevin was confronted directly, for the first time, with a topic at least as controversial and certainly more divisive than either attempted political interference or Church sensitivity—the role of RTÉ in promoting the Irish language. At a meeting of the Authority on 23 January 1964 a number of members demanded that Kevin investigate the absence of bilingual continuity, the failure of a host to contribute even short phrases in Irish and the interjection of songs in English between a recent programme on the Gaeltacht and *An Nuacht*.[198] It represented the beginning of a concentrated effort on the part of some members of the Authority to push the Irish language question to the top of the RTÉ agenda.

A new Authority was appointed in early 1965, for an initial one-year term. Its appointment gave further impetus to the Irish language cause. The focus of the Irish language lobby on the new Authority, particularly that of Donall O'Morain, Chairman of Gael Linn, Ruaidhri Brugha, an enthusiastic supporter of the language, and Filis Bean Ui Ceallaigh, widow of the former President of Ireland Sean T. O'Kelly, moved to the necessity of having an Irish person as Controller of Programmes. This in turn led to a sustained campaign against Gunnar Rugheimer, whose 'foreign-ness' was blamed for the failure of RTÉ to promote the Irish language adequately. At a meeting of the Authority in January 1965, Kevin urged that Rugheimer's foreign background should not be seen by the Authority as preventing him from sharing the Authority's objectives. Kevin argued that the Authority should feel that it was making appreciable contributions to the revival of Irish, even if that contribution were less than dedicated enthusiasts might desire.[199]

Kevin's plea for tolerance largely fell on deaf ears. In June 1965 Mr Brugha complained about the inadequacy of Irish-

Kevin on the right, aged one, with his brother Brendan.

Rugby training at Blackrock College.

Kevin in Kuala Lumpur in 1954 on one of his extensive export selling trips.

The Board of P.J. Carroll & Co. in 1956, with Kevin standing on the left, Don Carroll beside him in the centre and Arthur Cox seated second from the left.

St Patrick's Day 1956, in London with Michael Scott, Eamon Andrews and Cyril Cusack.

Before leaving Ireland for Holland in 1959 with Steve Rich of Hunter Douglas on the right and John McConnell of McConnell's Advertising Agency in the centre.

Returning to Ireland in 1963 to join RTÉ with Charles Brennan and Eamon Andrews of the RTÉ Authority.

Kevin in the background as President Kennedy says farewell to Sinéad Bean de Valera at the US Embassy.

With President de Valera and the director generals of European broadcasting services including, on Kevin's left, Jacques-Bernard Dupont of ORTF in France and, on his right, Sir Hugh Carleton Greene of the BBC.

The hands-on Chairman: at RTÉ in 1967.

With Tod Andrews, then Chairman of the RTÉ Authority in 1966.

With friends from the Smurfit Board, 1994. Standing left to right: Peter Gleeson, Kevin, James O'Dwyer. Seated left to right: Jack Lynch, Eoin Ryan, Billy McDonald.

With Edna O'Brien in 1974 (top) and at the Irish Distillers Head Office in Bow Street with Terry Wogan, Archie Cook and Richard Burrows.

Kevin in 1974 with his good friends Karl and Doreen Mullen and Peter Owens.

On site with Irish Steel at Hawlbowline.

The Board of Irish Distillers at Cork in 1984. From left: Richard Burrows, Aleck Crichton, Frank O'Reilly, Dorothie Richardson (Company Secretary), Michael Killeen, John A. Ryan, Ronnie Murphy, Gerald de Geoffre, Kevin McCourt, Shane Jameson, Jack Lynch, Nigel Beamish, Major Ronnie Robertson, Charles Neill, Clem Ryan, Gene Savage and Stephen Murphy.

With President Patrick Hillery and John Mooney of Gorta in 1986.

With Taoiseach Charles Haughey in 1989 (top) and with David Frost and Paddy Wright (below).

Receiving a presentation from Michael Smurfit on retirement from the Smurfit Board.

With Tom O'Higgins in Mayo in 1983.

In 1971 with Peggy, at his daughter Pamela's wedding in Rome.

With his son Declan after a good day's fishing on Lough Conn in 1964 and with his daughter Pamela (below).

At home in Eglinton Road, with Deirdre in 1989 (above) and Germaine in 1997.

Kevin as grandfather. Fishing in Waterville with Cian and Conal, Declan's sons (above) and with Pamela's children, Candida and Orson in Rome.

Kevin's favourite photo of his grandchildren. Back from left: Jonathan Staunton, Orson Francescone, Cian McCourt, Melanie and Conal McCourt. Front from left: Deborah Staunton, Melissa McCourt, Caroline Staunton, Mark Staunton, Candida Francescone.

Harmony Cottage, Kevin and Peggy's home from 1969.

speaking newscasters 'whose dialects rendered them unacceptable in certain parts of the country'.[200]

The battlelines were firmly drawn by October 1965, when the renewal of Rugheimer's contract came up for consideration by the Authority. At its meeting on 6 October the Authority expressed a wish that an Irishman with the necessary experience and professionalism be found for the position. This was stated not to be a denigration of Rugheimer's personal and professional qualifications. A motion was passed that said: 'Radio Éireann is a national service and its aim is a programme that will have a distinctively Irish quality and will reflect and cherish traditional Irish values.'[201] Mr O'Morain could not agree and asked that it be recorded that 'in the context of the minimal amount of Irish used in TV programmes since the establishment of the service, he regarded the statement as inadequate and could not subscribe to it.'[202]

The opposition to Rugheimer among members of the Authority was mirrored by a growing anti-'foreign' sentiment directed against him by the Gaelic League and by some newspapers. Most pointedly, a group of RTÉ producers, some at senior level, sent a letter to the Authority on 18 October 1965 in which they complained about a number of matters, including Rugheimer, who, they argued, dictated the content of programme schedules 'without the leavening influence of those who have a life-long understanding of national ideals and the Irish way of life'.[203] While the Authority refused to respond to the letter, two days after its receipt it resolved that the position of Controller of Programmes be advertised.

In December 1965 Gay Byrne, the compere of the station's flagship *Late Late Show*, incurred the wrath of Donall O'Morain, who complained about remarks Byrne had made in the Christmas edition of his show in relation to the Irish language revival, which O'Morain viewed as having been 'quite contrary to the recent policy affirmed by the Authority'.[204] Kevin rallied to Byrne's cause and persuaded a majority of the Authority's members that it was essential to good broadcasting to maintain freedom of debate and that the incident was not offensive to Authority policy.

The complaint about Gay Byrne was only one of a constant stream of objections raised by certain members of the Authority, who viewed meetings of the Authority as opportunities to offer guidance to the management on the proper use of the Irish language, such as advising that the Irish commentary on *Leargas* and *Ceamara na Cruinne* be delivered at a slower pace to allow for wider understanding.[205]

In January 1966 the Authority adopted a major policy statement on the language, which had as its foundation that RTÉ 'has a national responsibility to nurture the Irish language by presenting it in a sympathetic/positive and imaginative way.'[206]

The campaign against Rugheimer continued unabated. At a meeting of the Authority in April 1966, when Kevin reported on the lack of an obvious Irish candidate for the Programme Controller role, members of the Authority retorted that the challenge of the position could be offered to a candidate whose 'love for and knowledge of Ireland was not necessarily matched by the technical and managerial qualities of other candidates from outside the country. It was an insult to Ireland and to the Authority for staff to suggest that an Irish Controller could not be found.'[207]

The heated exchanges at that meeting in April 1966 would prove the last straw—not for Rugheimer, who would remain with the station until the end of the year, but for Eamonn Andrews. Five days after the meeting he wrote to the Taoiseach informing him of his intention to resign as Chairman. While expressing some annoyance at the manner in which the new Authority had been constituted in 1965 and was now to be reappointed *en bloc*, Andrews firmly lay the reason for his resignation at the door of the Irish language issue:

> I'm afraid the Authority as now constituted is too susceptible to outside pressure, principally on the score of the Irish language. Believe me, I recognise the problems you and the Government face in this area, and I have tried to compromise to the point beyond which honesty will not permit me to go. I fear very much that if present RTE policies in this respect are pursued, the service will get so far ahead of public acceptance that it will lose the Irish viewer to cross channel services as happened in radio. I already have distressing evidence of repercussions within the organisation itself. For the most sincere reasons, some members are pressing an unrealistic policy which I believe may have both artistic and financial repercussions of an unfortunate kind.[208]

On the same day he wrote to the Minister for Post and Telegraphs, Joseph Brennan:

> I longed to give to the country a strong virile and national television service, but it's just not possible in the present circumstances. At a time when I'm trying to get back home myself, I recoil from being involved in an exercise that I know in the ultimate will contribute to driving more of our own people away.[209]

At the request of the Taoiseach, Andrews kept his decision private until late May 1966, to give the Government time to choose his successor. On 24 May, faced with extensive media speculation both in Ireland and, due to his own high profile, in

England, Andrews released a statement confirming his resignation. He again underlined the role played by the disagreements on the revival of the Irish language and the qualification requirements for the Programme Controller in his decision:

> I have felt for some time past that in our projected Irish language programming we were in danger of moving too far ahead of our audience's capacity to maintain communication with us.
>
> I felt also that we in the television service would have less danger of slowing down our development if we continued for some time in the future to be courageous in finding some skilled people to help us from other countries.
>
> I found that I tended to hold views different from a number of my colleagues, in some cases from the majority of them, on these two important questions of communication and expertise. I felt in conscience that I could no longer lend myself to policies with which I could not agree and which I believed to be a danger to the service.[210]

Kevin was extremely upset by Andrews' decision to resign. They had developed an excellent working relationship, and he and Peggy had become close personal friends of Andrews and his wife, Grainne. On 30 May 1966 he wrote to Eamonn Andrews in the following terms:

> This last year has been a confused and straining one; the last few weeks were a sad and disappointing climax to it all.
>
> Over the weekend, I have had a hundred post mortems with myself, visualising every conceivable permutation of circumstances and wondering how I might the better have

advised you and the Authority – wondering how could I have averted a conclusion personally dismaying to me, bad for broadcasting, and I know, hurtful to you.

I have gone back over the Minutes, reconstructing the mood and circumstances of each meeting, but could only conclude that, in a series of situations no chief executive could have hoped to handle with perfection, I did and said within the limitations of my talent what was best at the time and in the circumstances ruling.

All that said, I want to hark back to our first meting late in 1962. While I had been flirting during that year with the thought of returning to Ireland, I was in no hurry about it and decided very carefully to pick my opportunity. Broadcasting of itself, although immediately attractive to me, would not have been the vehicle of my return; the premium attaching to your invitation was the fact that you were Chairman and my conviction after several meetings that I could develop a rapport officially and personally with you which would give me the security, support and professional guidance essential to my making at least some success of a difficult job.

I have never had one moment over the last three and a half years to regret my decision; on the contrary, as the organisation grew in size and complexity, the benefit of access to your wisdom and good judgment was enhanced by the privilege of your friendship and the often needed relief of your good humour. For a chief executive, it was the ideal relationship with the person who was the Chairman.

What has been said publicly of your contribution to broadcasting in Ireland is quite inadequate but – as with Wren – 'si monumentum requiris, circumspice'. An organisation is as good as its leadership permits it to be and

> the progress of television in an outstandingly short period of time is a credit on your balance sheet. In spite of our shortcomings – and I know them – I believe that no state body in the forty years of our freedom in Ireland has made such a progress so fast at such little cost to the community and with such a payoff back to the community in performance. This is your achievement. This and the sound principles of good broadcasting which you have instilled in me and others who will strive to preserve them in the future. Time will emphasise and clarify your contribution amongst even the sceptics – it can hardly add more conviction to my appreciation of three and a half years under your Chairmanship.
>
> For the knowing of you and Grainne and Eamma and Fergal we – all of my family – are grateful and intend that it will be a continuing warmth for us in the future.[211]

Andrews replied that he hoped that 'despite all the stupidity and shortsightedness you will not be lost to broadcasting … Your feel for and knowledge of the medium is remarkable … it will have been worth it all in so far as it brought the McCourts and the Andrews together. Your family is a greater tribute to you than all your undoubted professional success.'[212]

Andrews had previously recalled the occasion when he and his Director-General had been criticised heavily for something totally unavoidable, and Kevin gave him cause to smile by sending him a quote from Edmund Burke:

> Those who would carry on great public schemes must be proof against the worst fatiguing delays, the most mortifying disappointments, the most shocking insults and, worst of all, the presumptuous judgment of the ignorant upon their designs.[213]

Although Eamonn Andrews was an excellent broadcaster, Kevin recognised that his friend had severe limitations where business matters were concerned. 'He [Andrews] was not a good businessman,' Kevin later wrote, 'he had no experience of the politicking of business, its power struggles, its inherent resentments, ambitions, unkindness, selfishnesses, its cunning and manoeuvrings.'[214]

Not everyone was disappointed by Andrews' decision to resign as Chairman of the Authority. A letter-writer to the *Irish Press* declared:

> According to Mr. Andrews, the Telefís Éireann chairman, foreigners should continue to be brought in to tell us what programmes we should have and what we should not. After six years in which to train our own native staff, what kind of nonsense is this?
>
> Of course, there are none so blind as those that will not see. Mr. Andrews' sight may well be clouded by his long sojourn across the water. Undoubtedly there are skilled television men over there as there are in other countries – but sorry, Mr. Andrews, you're 50 years too late. Good men died 50 years ago so that we might now be free to run our own affairs here.[215]

Another correspondent proclaimed:

> What programmes in Irish are there? There's *Daithi Lacha* for five minutes (before six when few of us are home) There's *Nuacht* at 11.20 when many of us are in bed (or should be). And that's all. What, in the name of Moses is Eamonn Andrews talking about? Surely he doesn't mean the few words of Irish the little announcer girls speak?[216]

The Authority, for its part, formally asked Eamonn Andrews to reconsider his position, later expressing regret that he had included the Irish language as a reason for the conflict leading to his decision to resign. One member used the opportunity to declare that Rugheimer's contract was being terminated not merely on the basis of his Irish language qualifications but because of his 'diminished capacity, as a non-national, to have an appropriate feeling for programmes'.[217]

Many years later Rugheimer recalled Kevin as having been 'a very brave man on this issue. He sat down and discussed the matter with Conradh na Gaeilge who were abusive and negative.'[218]

The beginning of 1966, prior to Eamonn Andrews' resignation, had witnessed a number of events that would pass into RTÉ folklore. Preparations for the celebrations to mark the fiftieth anniversary of the 1916 Rising had begun over a year earlier. The fact that many who had been directly involved in the Rising were still alive, and some in high office, inevitably led to close scrutiny of the proposed content of the programmes. In July 1965 members of the Authority expressed concern at the use of the word 'rebellion' in relation to the events of 1916, while others objected to the suggestion that David Thornley, a Labour Party sympathiser, would contribute a lecture on Patrick Pearse.[219] It was felt that cynicism, and even analysis, should be avoided and emphasis placed instead on the 'idealism' of the Rising. There was a general feeling that the series should be approached in an 'imaginative and grand' manner and should include a central commemorative event, 'evocative of the stirring events of the week of the Rising'.[220] At an Authority meeting shortly before the series was broadcast, Mr Brugha warned of likely criticism at the failure to feature Éamon de Valera in the series, while Michael Collins was featured in six episodes. Kevin explained that this was the result of production sensitivity at casting a live person and, in particular, the President of Ireland.[221]

Kevin recalled that at a private viewing of part of the series before it was broadcast publicly, one member of the Authority was seen to cry. Another member, Bean Ui Cheallaigh, who had been in the GPO in Easter Week 1916, was according to Kevin, 'composed about it and yet very upset because it did not depict it as she remembered it, or thought she remembered it or how she would like it to be remembered'.[222] Later, at an Authority meeting, she complained of a number of historical inaccuracies that, in her view, could have been avoided had her suggestion of consultation with 1916 survivors been taken up in the planning stages.[223]

The series, entitled *Insurrection*, produced by Louis Lentin and directed by Michael Garvey, was well received at home and became the first major export sale of an Irish television series: the entire series was shown in Britain and Australia, with some of the programmes broadcast in Canada, Sweden, Holland, Belgium, Finland and Denmark.

The RTÉ 'event' of 1966 was not the meticulously planned *Insurrection* series, however, nor even the sudden resignation of the Chairman of the Authority. On 12 February 1966 the *Late Late Show* played host to an innocuous quiz in which a husband and wife were asked questions about each other's habits, with prizes awarded depending on how well a couple could answer the questions. Amid general high spirits and laughter, one wife, whose husband was having difficulty recalling the colour of the nightdress she had worn on her wedding night, intervened to suggest that she had in fact worn none.

A scandalised Bishop Tom Ryan of Clonfert telephoned the *Sunday Press* to say that he intended to preach to his flock in Loughrea the following morning about the 'objectionable'[224] content of the programme, and that he would be asking his people not to watch the show again. The host of the show, Gay

Byrne, expressed the view that he was 'at a loss to know why there should be any objection from anyone'.[225] Despite extensive coverage of the Bishop's complaints in the Sunday papers, Byrne remained relaxed, particularly after a social encounter with Gunner Rugheimer, who dismissed the controversy as intensely funny and another indication of the quaintness of the Irish mind.[226]

The story would not go away, however. On the Monday after the show was aired, *The Irish Times* had as its leading headline 'The Bishop and the Nightie',[227] and this was how the affair would for all time be remembered. The Loughrea Town Commissioners, the Mayo GAA Board and the Meath VEC, among others, joined with provincial newspapers across the country to condemn the *Late Late Show* and its young host. The *Irish Catholic* referred to 'the growing tendency to play down the grave implications of the Sixth and Ninth Commandments and the unworthy part that Telefís Éireann, deliberately or unthinkingly, is taking in that process.'[228]

Rugheimer's initial dismissal of the controversy as quaint dissipated as the story grew and grew. He and Kevin met with Byrne, who later described them as 'agitated' and insistent that a statement be issued acknowledging that the programme had been embarrassing to a section of its viewers. 'Why they wanted to do this was never very clear to me,' Byrne later wrote, 'but I got the distinct impression that there was a bad case of the screaming funks going around, and everybody was catching it fast.'[229]

Archbishop McQuaid, for his part, wisely avoided becoming embroiled in the public debate, but he wrote privately to Kevin at his home address, more in sorrow than anger, to describe the offending questions and answers on the programme as 'vulgar, even coarse and suggestive'. He declared: 'You [Kevin] have not been fairly treated,' he declared, 'for this type of thing is quite unlike what you have been warmly thanked for.'[230]

Kevin replied:

> ... the generosity and kindness of your letter about last Saturday's Late Late Show moved me to distress that you should have had cause at all to write on such a matter. Television possesses some magnetism for risk-taking and for being racy, especially in the field of light entertainment. But be assured, please, that I do not tolerate the tawdry, the deprecation of what I believe to be the inherent good taste and instincts of Irish people. Not infrequently to my frustration, I cannot be the policeman of all I want and still manage a large and complex organisation; but the mistakes, believe me, stem more from inexperience, enthusiasm and bad judgement rather than from malice or misery of outlook.[231]

At a meeting of the Authority two weeks after the broadcast, Kevin sought to play down the incident as an error of judgment. The Authority, no doubt conscious of the increasing commercial importance to the station of Byrne and his programme, accepted Kevin's view and resolved that there 'was no cause for official chastisement of the producer [Byrne]'.[232] It expressed the wish, however, that he should have full regard in the future to the need to uphold the standards of Irish taste in presenting the programme and hoped that a similar deviation would not occur again.

The desire for a controversy-free *Late Late Show* was to be in vain. In the week before the 'Bishop and the Nightie' furore, Gay Byrne had sought to have Victor Lownes as a guest on the programme. Lownes was in Ireland to recruit fifty girls to join a Bunny Club being opened in London. McQuaid had also raised this issue with Kevin, declaring it as something 'you would not, I think, let into the house'. Kevin replied that he had arranged for Lownes' appearance to be cancelled as soon as he had become aware of it.

Less than two months after the 'Bishop and the Nightie' furore, the programme was again in trouble with the hierarchy when one of its guests, a Trinity College student, Brian Trevaskis, described the new Cathedral in Galway as 'a ghastly monstrosity', the Bishop of Galway as 'a moron' and Archbishop McQuaid as someone who 'has put back the image of Ireland from fifty to one hundred years'.[233]

As with the previous incident, there was no shortage of expressions of outrage, even though Bishop Browne of Galway issued what was, in the circumstances, a temperate if strident defence of his position. Trevaskis appeared on the *Late Late Show* again the following week to apologise for his remarks, but only succeeded in causing further outrage by saying that while the Bishop of Galway clearly knew the meaning of the word 'moron', he doubted whether he knew the meaning of the word 'Christianity'. Kevin issued a detailed statement in which he regretted the 'disparaging' remarks in relation to the Bishop of Galway and the 'unkind' reference to the Archbishop of Dublin. He did, however, defend the programme in as strong terms as might have been possible:

> The Late Late Show is unscripted and unrehearsed. In any other form it may fail on its purpose as a spontaneous television programme of discussion and entertainment. Those invited to take part are chosen in the belief that they will contribute in a fair-minded way to the enjoyment and interest of the programme; their opinions do not necessarily have to be popular opinions.

> In a programme of this kind one takes a risk that, in the heat of argument or because of an error of judgment, a participant may err in a departure from good taste or in ungracious reference to individuals.
>
> The Late Late Show has been on the air for a period of over four years and has established itself as a successful television programme with wide public acceptance. Without discounting their undesirability, breaches such as those referred to have been few. The producer-compere of the show is fully aware of my concern that standards of taste and courtesy are maintained at all times.[234]

At the next Authority meeting Kevin again defended the *Late Late Show* and refuted suggestions that 'an undesirable trend had crept into the programme'.[235] He found himself, once more, in correspondence with Archbishop McQuaid in relation to the programme, writing to him on 5 April 1966 to express his 'great embarrassment and appreciable anger'[236] at what had occurred.

The person appointed to replace Eamonn Andrews as Chairman of the Authority was Dr C.S. (Tod) Andrews, who had considerable experience in the public service having been managing director of Bord na Móna and Chairman of CIÉ. He was very different in belief and style from his predecessor. He felt that RTÉ should do more to promote the use of Irish language in everyday communication. Within days of his arrival, he summoned all the staff to a meeting in the canteen and declared that, in future, there should be at least one Irish language phrase in each programme. Gay Byrne, who attended the meeting, recalls Kevin sitting in complete silence, looking mortified.[237] Tod Andrews strongly believed that the station was, as Lemass would later describe it, 'an instrument of public policy and as such responsible to Government'.²³⁸ This view, Tod Andrews later wrote, was borne from 'very definite and sometimes sorry experiences of the consequences of resistance to government policies by some of the semi-State bodies and even by civil servants.'²³⁹ The arrival of Tod Andrews therefore made significantly more challenging the efforts Kevin had been making since his arrival to ensure RTÉ remained free from political interference.

Tod Andrews had a very different style in the chair from his namesake. While Eamonn Andrews encouraged, or at least tolerated, lengthy discussions at Authority meetings and at times struggled to maintain discipline around the table, Tod Andrews directed that detailed papers be circulated in advance, so that, as far as possible, decisions could be taken at meetings on a 'yes' or 'no' basis. He also changed the frequency of meetings from two to just one per month. The minutes of meetings were restricted to records of decisions made rather than records of the debate that had taken place, as had been the practice in Eamonn Andrews' time. He ended the practice of recording the observations of Authority members on topics such as the Irish language or programming issues in favour of noting that suggestions had been made and that the Director-General should take action, where appropriate, in relation to them.

The relationship between Kevin and Tod Andrews was one of mutual respect, but it lacked the personal warmth and regard that was a major feature of the relationship between Kevin and Eamonn Andrews. Tod Andrews later described Kevin as a man of 'integrity and decency', of 'tolerance and kindness', who by 'hard work and laudable ambition … had ascended the commercial ladder', but he also pointedly described the difference between them:

I liked and respected Kevin McCourt (as we say, he hadn't a bad turn in him) but unlike him my roots were deeply in the public service. I was probably more critical of some of its procedures than most but I had long since accepted the proposition that there were no rewards to be expected from hard work or success even if there was no punishment for those who failed to make the grade.[240]

Kevin later recalled Tod Andrews as 'a very strong personality, the archetypal public servant, with a tremendous track record, not only independence but singlemindedness, extremes of tolerance and intolerance, a man of great humanity. A man who, when you got to know him, denied his outward irascibility and impatience with great sentimentality and heart.'[241]

The Presidential election held in June 1966 witnessed a very close race between the incumbent, the eighty-three-year-old Éamon de Valera and T.F. O'Higgins of Fine Gael. Kevin regarded the election as a political event, therefore RTÉ offered time for party political broadcasts on behalf of each candidate. President de Valera's Director of Elections, Charles Haughey, complained that the President was above politics and could not participate, whereupon Kevin retorted that the President could have others speak on his behalf, but that the invitation to O'Higgins stood. Yet it was O'Higgins, narrowly defeated in the election, who later complained about how RTÉ had behaved. Speaking in the Dáil in March 1969, O'Higgins claimed that the Authority had issued a directive to Kevin that no news of any part of the campaign was to be broadcast because only one candidate was campaigning.[242] He also claimed that Kevin had been directed to publicise fully any appearances by the President, but to ignore briefings given on behalf of O'Higgins. On reading media reports of the speech, Kevin—by now gone from RTÉ—wrote to O'Higgins, a neighbour and close friend of his (the two families had holidayed together in the west of Ireland), denying that he had received any orders or directions, as Director-General, in relation to the broadcasting of the campaign.[243]

In September 1966 the Authority, on Kevin's recommendation, appointed an insider, Michael Garvey, to succeed Rugheimer as Controller of Programmes. It was to prove a popular appointment. Garvey was viewed not only as an outstanding producer but in the eyes of many he had the added 'advantage' of being fluent in the Irish language.

The year 1966 ended with further allegations of political interference. While in all previous cases Kevin had succeeded in walking the thin line between seeking to diffuse the situation with a diplomatic apology and, at the same time, robustly defending the independence of his RTÉ and its staff, on this occasion he was to find himself in open disagreement with many of his colleagues.

On 1 October 1966 Charles Haughey, now Minister for Agriculture, telephoned the RTÉ newsroom to complain about the manner in which a statement he had made in relation to agricultural prices had been juxtaposed with a contrary statement on the same topic by a leader of the National Farmers' Association (NFA), Richard Deasy. At the time, the Minister and the Government were embroiled in a very difficult and public battle with the main farming organisations over agricultural prices. Following Haughey's intervention the NFA statement was omitted from subsequent bulletins—a decision that infuriated the National Union of Journalists.

By chance, Kevin was due to speak to members of the Dublin Chamber of Commerce two days later on the topic 'Broadcasting—a Public Service'. In his address, Kevin strongly asserted that broadcasting remained independent of political and other interference:

> The broadcasting service is statutorily independent; not being a Government department, it is free of interference in, or direction as to its daily affairs; it enjoys absolute control and the exercise of its own judgment over editorial content.
>
> There is a great deal of nonsense talked about the broadcasting service being the tool of this party or that, being the prejudiced protagonist of one point of view or the antinational antagonist of another. I have never known that a programme has been changed or withdrawn or made as the result of political or any other kind of pressure.[244]

In relation to recent events, he added:

> I must refer to press reports yesterday and today about a recent news item. There is neither mystery nor intrigue involved in this. We made an error of editorial judgment. When this happens, I hope we would always have both the courage and the judgment to correct it. The head of news discovered immediately after the news bulletin – it should have been discovered before it – that there was an error. It was corrected in succeeding bulletins. I fully support the action he took on it.
>
> We have no right to hurt the feelings of people, nor have we the wish to set ourselves up as the judges of what is good for our society and what it should have indifferent to its ability to absorb it. It is not our aim to cater for the avant garde, to shoot for ultra sophistication. One of the advantages of the country is that we are not an ultra-sophisticated people and I hope we never will be.

> If we make a blunder and an occasional expression of bad taste, believe me we blush for it and do try to learn a lesson from it.[245]

The next day's newspapers ran with headlines emphasising that Kevin had accepted that RTÉ had made an 'error of editorial judgment'. They also covered, in some detail, the strongly worded rejection of Kevin's statement that was issued by the Dublin Radio branch of the National Union of Journalists:

> The branch has seen the remarks of the Director-General of Radio Telefis Éireann, Mr. Kevin McCourt, at the Dublin Chamber of Commerce today regarding the complaint of Mr. Haughey, Minister for Agriculture and Fisheries, to the News Division last week.
>
> The branch disagrees with the Director-General's assertion that an error of editorial judgment was made (at chief sub-editor level) in regard to the broadcast of the N.F.A. statement on Thursday with politics; it is concerned with fair and accurate news and with the professional integrity of its members. The branch would now like a clear statement by the Authority on its news policy and gives an assurance to the public that no one can expect the willing co-operation of members of this union in presenting 'managed' or 'doctored' news.
>
> We accept the right of the Director-General and the Head of News to make final judgment on news bulletins, even though we disagree with their decisions, but we cannot now stand by and hear the Director-General declare publicly that the error of judgment on Thursday night was made not by the Head of News in withdrawing the N.F.A. statement but by the editorial staff in giving it.[246]

Kevin found himself also under attack from the NFA, which used the episode to further its campaign against the Minister and to extend support to the NUJ:

> This most recent attempt by the Minister for Agriculture and Fisheries to hinder the democratic right of freedom of speech is but one further example of the arrogance of Mr. Haughey. It is an episode which calls for the severest censure both from his colleagues in the Government and from the Irish public.
>
> At the same time nothing but the highest of admiration must be expressed to the members of the National Union of Journalists who had the courage to bring this whole matter out into the open, where the public can make their own assessment.[247]

Kevin's attempt to diffuse the situation through his Dublin Chamber speech cut no ice with *The Irish Times,* which declared the following day, in an editorial headed 'Run for Cover':

> Mr. Kevin McCourt's apologia before the Dublin Chamber of Commerce reads oddly, particularly in conjunction with the statement from the members of the National Union of Journalists who work in his organisation. Had Mr. McCourt said simply: 'Of course there exists pressure and interference and of course we resist strenuously', he would have been on firmer ground as head of a national service. To argue in a circuitous way that pressures do not exist for his staff or that they have no effect is nonsense in the present circumstances. There must be politicians today laughing like cats at the thought that their verbal assaults on senior personnel in Telefís Éireann do not, in the opinion of the Director-General, amount to interference.

One would like to feel that there was a bit more steel in the members of the Authority and their senior servants in Montrose – if Mr. McCourt has presented the picture as others around him see it too. The officials have only their jobs to lose if it comes to a fight and no doubt a golden handshake from Montrose is something worthwhile.

The members of the National Union of Journalists who belong to the radio and television branch have, perhaps not without envy, been described as rather cosseted, and the implication has been there that they were perhaps as much civil servants as journalists. In this case they have stood up well for their rights, and the public should be grateful to them. Mr. McCourt could not over-estimate the value of word being passed from mouth to mouth at Montrose that on the occasion of the next imperious telephone call the answer had been 'Tell the Minister to go to hell'.[248]

The complaint by Haughey to the newsroom and Kevin's attempt to diffuse the situation were far from the end of the matter. Another row erupted with Haughey over a decision to invite Deasy to debate with Haughey on the current affairs programme, *Division*. Haughey claimed that convention required that only elected members of the Oireachtas could appear on the programme. The programme's producer, Muiris MacConghail, recalled the Director-General's office as 'being under siege'[249] at the time, but that Kevin held his nerve and supported Rugheimer and MacConghail in their efforts to guarantee, as far as possible, impartiality notwithstanding Haughey's obdurate stance.

The controversy led directly to Lemass making a blunt, oft-quoted statement in Dáil Éireann on 12 October, in which he described RTÉ as 'an instrument of public policy':

The Government have overall responsibility for its conduct and especially the obligation to ensure that its programmes do not offend against the public interest or conflict with national policy as defined in legislation. To this extent the government reject the view that Radio Telefís Éireann should be, either generally or in regard to its current affairs programmes, completely independent of Government supervision.[250]

Eventually the stand-off between RTÉ and the Government was resolved. A meeting in the Shelbourne Hotel, attended by Kevin, Tod Andrews and Erskine Childers, by now Minister for Posts and Telegraphs, allowed the Government a further opportunity to express its dissatisfaction.

Within a month of his Dáil speech, Lemass had been replaced as Taoiseach by Jack Lynch, who would prove less consumed by media comment than his predecessor. Childers also played his part, assuring Lynch that there was no inherent anti-Fianna Fáil bias in RTÉ:

Andrews tells me that between the Board and the staff the idea that there is not sufficient Fianna Fáil support in RTE is ludicrous. McCourt has endless conflicts with Fine Gael and Labour.[251]

The public disagreement between Kevin and the NUJ arising from the Haughey/NFA saga undoubtedly affected his standing among certain RTÉ journalists, who had viewed Kevin, up to that time, as an unswerving ally in the cause of journalistic independence from political interference. The unequivocal assertion by Lemass that RTÉ was an instrument of Government policy added further to their dismay.

The public affairs section of RTÉ's programme division

fought back, making broadcasting independence a news story in itself. Leading international broadcasters, including Walter Cronkite of CBS, lent their support to a *7 Days* feature on the topic. The issue simply would not go away and would dominate Kevin's remaining time at RTÉ.

In early 1967 a decision was taken to send a news team to North Vietnam to cover the conflict there. It was a decision that had Kevin's full support and encouragement. He saw the venture as 'a highly imaginative exercise'.[252] The proposal also found favour with the Authority.

The Government proved much less enthusiastic, however. The Minister for External Affairs, Frank Aiken, voiced strenuous objections to his Cabinet colleague, Erskine Childers. They were convinced that a visit by an RTÉ crew would be damaging to Irish interests, primarily with the United States. These concerns were put before the Authority, which reversed its previous decision and decided against sending a crew to North Vietnam.

The revised decision by the Authority followed a conversation between the Taoiseach and the Chairman of the Authority. Speaking later in the Dáil, Lynch confirmed that he had:

> ... recently informed the Chairman of Radio Telefis Éireann that, in the opinion of the Government the best interests of the nation would not be served by sending a news team to Vietnam, as proposed by the Authority and that such a visit would be an embarrassment to the Government in relation to its foreign policy.[253]

The basis on which the Government felt compelled to make its views known to the Authority was that RTÉ was a semi-State body and that 'if a team representing Radio Telefis Eireann went to Vietnam, the peculiar character of a semi-State body, as we know it, could well be misinterpreted all over the world.'[254]

For his part, Tod Andrews later acknowledged that 'the proper course to follow would have been to insist that if the government wanted the project abandoned they should exercise their statutory powers by issuing a formal instruction to this effect', but he decided against this course in favour of the compromise of a conversation with the Taoiseach, which, he later admitted, was 'an error of judgement'.[255]

The reaction of staff was one of fury. In their view, their concern that the events of the previous year were evidence of an intention on the part of the Government to erode the independence of RTÉ and an acquiescence on the part of the Authority and management to this erosion was proving to be a valid one. The NUJ demanded a meeting with the Taoiseach, Jack Lynch. When this was rejected, over 100 members of staff, who were not members of the NUJ, signed a letter to the Taoiseach complaining about the decision to cancel the Vietnam coverage:

> The undersigned employees of Radio Telefís Éireann protest in the strongest terms as to the action of the Government in relation to RTÉ's proposed coverage of Vietnam. We urgently request the Taoiseach and the Government to reconsider the machinery by which the cancellation of this project was effected.
>
> We consider that such action strikes dangerously at responsible broadcasting and at the dissemination of objective news.[256]

It was now the Authority's turn to feel annoyed. Kevin later recalled that the decision by staff to bypass the Authority and management and air their grievances directly to the Taoiseach caused the whole Authority to 'erupt in resentment'[257] at what its members viewed as defiance and disrespect. On 1 May 1967

Kevin issued a memorandum to all staff in which, having denied political interference, he bluntly declared that staff were not entitled to criticise the Authority in public:

> In view of the recent widespread publicity given to the cancellation of the proposal to send a News team to Vietnam, I think it necessary to bring the following to the notice of all members of the staff.
>
> The Vietnam project was conceived and planned within the organisation as desirable in the interests of news and informative programming. The concept was an enterprising one and reflected a commendable desire within the organisation to concern itself with the major events and happenings in the present-day world. The decision to abandon the project was taken by the Authority after very careful consideration of the new circumstances brought to its notice. This decision was made by the Authority alone and there was no question of any infringement of the Authority's independence in programme matters being involved.
>
> The decisions of the Authority on broadcasting matters are binding on the staff of RTE, and the fact that certain members of the staff should have issued a public letter to the Taoiseach protesting in their capacity as employees of RTE at what was described in the letter as the action of the Government in relation to the Vietnam project is to be deplored. I must go on record to each member of the organisation that public criticism by members of the staff of a matter involving the governing body of the broadcasting service is inadmissible.
>
> The framework of the organisation has been shaped so as to provide as much communication as possible upwards and

downwards in an organisation of this size and complexity. There is adequate machinery for representations by the staff, primarily through the Divisional Heads, and in the more serious issues, direct on request to me. I think I do not have to assure you that responsible representations will always receive consideration, but I do insist on the observance by members of the staff of these proper organisational channels to the exclusion of others.[258]

Kevin's contract was due to expire at the end of 1967. The Authority was anxious that it be renewed and opened discussions with him a full year before the expiry date. At its meeting in December 1966, the Authority decided to recommend to the Minister that Kevin's contract be extended for a period of seven years from 1 January 1968 (which would have brought him close to his sixtieth birthday), at a salary of £6,500 per annum, to be adjusted biennially for cost of living increases and a representation allowance of £750 per annum. Despite reminders, no response was received from the Department until May 1967, when the Secretary of the Department indicated that while the Minister was favourably disposed to the continuance of Kevin's existing contract, any improvement in remuneration could only be considered in the context of a general review of top executive salaries of State companies then being undertaken.[259] The Authority was concerned with the inadequacy of the response and resolved that a delegation from the Authority should seek a meeting with the Taoiseach on the matter.[260]

The Minister did not formally consent to improved terms for Kevin until 8 December 1967, just three weeks before his existing contract was due to expire. It was too late. At a meeting of the Authority on the same day, Kevin announced that he had decided not to accept the offer of a new seven-year contract and that he would leave RTÉ at the end of March 1968.

Kevin may have hoped that his final months in the Director-General's chair would be uneventful, but the opposite proved to be the case. Shortly before he announced his decision to leave a dispute arose after Gay Byrne made direct approaches to the Taoiseach and several members of the Cabinet to appear on the *Late Late Show*. The Government rebuked these approaches. Under pressure, Kevin censured Byrne, although John Horgan noted that given Kevin's track record, the reprimand was likely to have been 'a mild one'.[261] When it was suggested at a meeting of the Programme Policy Committee that 'recent events are now encouraging the opinion that RTÉ is being run from underneath', Kevin acknowledged 'with some bitterness' that those views were 'not entirely unfounded'.[262]

In early 1968, just a few weeks before Kevin's departure date, an even greater drama unfolded. On 24 January, Kevin learned that a team from RTÉ had been invited to visit Biafra to report on the Civil War there. Biafra was a region in Nigeria in revolt against the Nigerian Government. The Biafra state was not recognised by Ireland or by many countries, with the exception of Portugal. Kevin telephoned the Secretary of the Department of External Affairs, Hugh McCann, and was told that any action by an official or quasi-official body from Ireland 'could be represented or misrepresented as partisan in the unfortunate conflict in Nigeria, could be detrimental to our people in one or other of the areas involved in the struggle and might even endanger their safety'.[263] To his dismay, Kevin then learned that three RTÉ personnel had already gone to Lisbon, on their way to Biafra, without his knowledge. Kevin immediately ordered them to return to Ireland.

The team involved in the proposed Biafran trip were

connected to the programme, *7 Days*, the station's flagship current affairs programme, to which Muiris MacConghail had recently been appointed as Producer. The programme team included a number of young, creative reporters and directors. In late 1967 and early 1968, *7 Days* had featured a number of hard-hitting stories, such as an interview with the property speculator Matt Gallagher, a programme described by one critic as a 'crudely-done disembowelment'.[264] Another feature, on Irish emigrants in Britain, provoked a response from a familiar source, Archbishop McQuaid, who complained that the programme included admissions by some of the emigrants that they did not go to Mass, a fact later verified by a group of London priests.

Prior to their departure for Biafra, the *7 Days* team had completed a feature on a controversial planning dispute at Mount Pleasant Square in Dublin, which was shelved by John Irvine in Kevin's absence, much to the annoyance of the team. An even more controversial programme was in gestation, involving an investigation into the activities of the Garda Special Branch, specifically surrounding the eviction and arrest of two members of the Communist Party; neither Kevin, as Director-General, nor Michael Garvey, as Controller of Programmes, had any prior knowledge of the proposed Special Branch programme. Indeed, to his considerable annoyance Kevin learned of the existence of the programme from a Government Minister. When Kevin viewed the film on 2 February he requested cuts—specifically of footage showing Dr Noël Browne being confronted by Garda dogs during a demonstration—but he approved of it being broadcast. The Chairman of the Authority, Tod Andrews, viewed the programme a few days later and thought it 'trivial and lightweight in content and unsuitable for transmission'.[265] He arranged to have the programme viewed by other members of the Authority. They came to the same conclusion and the programme was cancelled.

The Biafra and Special Branch episodes and, in particular, the fact that both occurred without Kevin's prior knowledge brought to a head a confrontation that had been simmering for months. Its roots may well have been in a sense of disillusionment on the part of some staff with Kevin's uncharacteristically autocratic missive in relation to the Vietnam incident and his public apology in relation to the NFA/Haughey saga—evidence of his failure, as they saw it, to defend broadcasting autonomy as he had in the past, as 'increasingly his resistance seemed to weaken'.[266] On Kevin's part, there was significant frustration at what he viewed as a lack of proper management control and irritation at the increasing level of dissent from within the staff ranks.

Kevin recognised that decisive action was required. In January, before either the Biafra or Special Branch issues had surfaced, the Head of News, Jim McGuinness, had raised the spectre of combining the Current Affairs and News Divisions, while at the same time acknowledging that it could prove 'an explosive possibility'. Kevin decided to do just that and in a curt message posted on RTÉ noticeboards on 12 February 1968 announced that ' …with effect from today, responsibility for public affairs programmes in television at present covered by 7 Days, will be transferred to the Head of the News Division'.[267]

All hell promptly broke loose!

A joint Union meeting instructed the staff concerned not to report for duty to McGuinness, a *7 Days* edition due for 13 February was blacked and had to be cancelled and six members of the *7 Days* staff were suspended, including the Producer, MacConghail, who, as he recounted later, 'was given an unusual assignment — to suspend myself'.[268] Later, three members of the

National Union of Journalists who had individual contracts indicated that they would report to Garvey but not to McGuinness and they, too, were suspended, drawing the NUJ into the fray. A union meeting voted by seventy-three votes to three in favour of industrial action and a complete shutdown of the station loomed.

The mood of at least some of the staff, in particular towards Kevin, was exemplified by a satirical piece—later dismissed by Tod Andrews as 'juvenilia'[269]—posted in the staff canteen:

> To All, Whether it concerns them or not:
>
> The Director-General wants to inform the staff that following controversial statements by Daithi Lacha, in the current series of programmes, he has decided to transfer responsibility for the series to Mr. Michael O'Hehir, head of sport. The reason for this change is a logical one in that the animals concerned have been known to run on occasions and would, therefore, fit more easily in the sports department. There was no question of interference with the head of children's programmes, who would still have full freedom to play the National Anthem at 5.30 pm every day.
>
> In regard to Quicksilver, it is confirmed that this programme will now be under the direct control of the Archbishop of Dublin, following the unfortunate slip of a competitor in using the word 'feck' on the programme. The Director-General wishes to deny that this change-over from money prizes to indulgences is an unwarranted intrusion in the affairs of the producer.
>
> The fact that the Late Late Show is now being transmitted without sound is one more example of the technical daring which makes Montrose the courageous leader of the Irish people. Fury without sound is a far more civilised form of

> entertainment. Should panellists continue to use untoward facial expressions, it is eventually intended to dispense with vision also …
>
> All those who still have opinions are advised to cash them in at the Chairman's office before 28 June when a referendum will be held.[270]

At a meeting of the Authority on 16 February, Kevin outlined the background to the dispute in much more sober terms. He said that since mid-1967 he had not been satisfied that there was fully effective editorial control of programmes in the programme division. He cited the Biafra and Special Branch episodes as examples of failure in communication, but said these were not isolated incidences. He informed the Authority that before making the decision to transfer, he had obtained the consent of both Michael Garvey and Jim McGuinness to do so, but that at the last moment Garvey had changed his mind about the proposal and had spoken of resigning if the transfer were made.

The Authority endorsed Kevin's actions in strong terms, issuing the following statement:

> At a meeting of the RTE Authority this morning, the actions taken by DG in relation to the 7 Days programme over the last few days were endorsed. It was noted that since the controversy arose consultation with Union officials has taken place from which it was clear that the real matter at issue is whether the DG or the staff had the right to decide who should be in charge of any programme or where in the organisation management of a programme should be located. In view of the fact that no authority, public or private, could yield on such a basis issue of management, the DG would suspend those members of the staff who now refuse to carry out their duties.

At the meetings with the Union officials, the DG indicated that no change in the character of the 7 Days programme was envisaged. In fact it is planned to extend one of the two weekly 7 Days programmes from thirty to forty five minutes from September next.

The Authority takes this occasion to assure the public that at no time has the Authority or the DG permitted outside pressures to influence their decisions contrary to their interpretation of their duties under the Broadcasting Authority Act.[271]

The reference in the Authority's statement to their decisions not being influenced by 'outside pressures' was a reaction to the suggestion in some media commentary that the moves in relation to *7 Days* were influenced by Government annoyance at an edition of the programme broadcast in December 1967, which asserted that if the Government's proposed referendum to abolish proportional representation as the method of election was successful, this would guarantee Fianna Fáil a huge majority. The Labour Party TD Frank Cluskey was widely reported as stating that the Biafra and Special Branch incidences were 'side issues' and that 'the main reason why the programme has been muzzled is largely due to the approach of the P.R. referendum'.[272]

As with all RTÉ controversies, the strike threat arising from the proposed *7 Days* transfer got very wide coverage. The written media, both in Ireland and England, were very critical of the handling of the affair. Terence de Vere White proclaimed that 'It may seem absurd that in any concern the workers should dictate policy to their director, but this matter has been ineptly handled.'[273] In its editorial of 21 February, headed 'Montrose emotion', *The Irish Times* opined:

> Modern management principles have their undeniable uses, but to adopt too much the principle of delegation in a communications structure, and then to find a crisis on your hands, shows the difference between a business organisation pure and simple and an organisation which deals largely in ideas and emotions.[274]

One piece of light relief in the coverage came when Michael Garvey explained to reporters that 'matters are in the hands of God', leading experienced Dublin sceptics to assume this was an error and that he was in fact referring to matters being 'in the hands of Tod'![275]

On 20 February, Kevin issued a newsletter to all staff explaining the reasons for the transfer of *7 Days* to the News Division, which were the same as those given to the Authority a week earlier, although while he cited the Biafra episode in the newsletter, he made no reference to the shelved Special Branch programme. By now RTÉ and the unions were involved in a conciliation process to resolve the dispute. On 29 February the Chairman of the Conciliation Mr T.K. Liston, S.C., made a series of recommendations, including that the *7 Days* team transfer, as a team, to the News Division. In early March management and unions accepted the recommendations and 'the evolution of RTE', as Tod Andrews put it, 'moved on a little'.[276]

Kevin, too, was moving on. While anxious not to leave RTÉ with the problem unresolved, Kevin had begun to consider whether an earlier than scheduled departure by him might actually help matters. He asked Muiris MacConghail to meet him in the Shelbourne Hotel,[277] which MacConghail did, accompanied by David Thornley. Over several drinks the three of them discussed the whole situation. By the end of the evening Kevin had decided to ask the Authority to allow him to leave immediately, rather than at the end of March. The Authority agreed to his request. Speaking many years later, Kevin recalled that he had 'the doubtful distinction of relinquishing my otherwise very happy time in RTE at the time of a major strike'.[278]

As events had transpired, while Kevin's career at RTÉ had been book-ended by industrial unrest, he had overseen enormous change and brought a sense of professionalism and order to the organisation. The Authority employed over 1,200 people. By 1967 its income was over £4 million, of which 56 per cent was advertising income, with the balance derived from licence fees. The Authority had produced a nett surplus over its seven years, deficits in radio (largely due to the external musical activity over and above broadcasting) being offset by surpluses on the television side. As Kevin left RTÉ, plans to introduce a colour television service were underway.

Looking back some years later, Kevin said:

> I like to think that I did bring organisation into RTÉ, in the sense that I brought deployed organisation, recruited some very good people, brought balance and a sense of cohesiveness into the inter-relations of the different functions of broadcasting.
>
> For the time I was there we always fulfilled our statutory obligation not to be a financial charge on the nation. But that was a secondary consideration to what I would like to think I succeeded in doing. We not only entertained. We used the facilities of broadcasting to advance specific aspects of the Irish way of life: the language, the place of religion – all religions in Ireland, the dignity of the home, the decency and quality of the Irish people and of the land of Ireland, tourism and the industry of Ireland.[279]

In a letter to John Irvine on the occasion of the latter's retirement from RTÉ in December 1975, Kevin once more recalled his own days at the national broadcaster:

> Not smugly but with much satisfaction, I think that maybe I had the best spell of the whole lot. Ed had a designing and building job and he must never have been totally secure in spirit in not being naturally of the Irish scene. I came at a time when it was all still a-growing, there was tremendous capacity for flexibility, mistakes were not grievous, people were enthusiastic, and I feel, more biddable than they later became, management was managing and there was a great air of creative enthusiasm about the place which, in retrospect, far outshone the intellectual experimentalists and the situation exploiters.
>
> Good days they were and I find it much easier to recall the successes and achievements and the happy occasions than I do the strains and pressures by which we must have been afflicted.[280]

Even among those staff who disagreed strongly with Kevin along the way, particularly in relation to his final act of moving *7 Days*, there was recognition of his business skills:

> Kevin McCourt was fastidious and dapper, gifted in organisational ability, a Daniel in money matters, and, according to those who knew him well, a man of charm, humour and imagination – and something of a dreamer. If he had an Achilles' heel, it was a certain sensitivity which may have laid him open, in his role as a representative of broadcasting, to the thin winds of Dublin society's backbiting gossip.
>
> He was an experienced and shrewd business adminis-

trator. When he was able to maintain the necessary stolid detachment, he was a good judge of people and their capabilities. Like many men whose experience was derived from the competitive field of commerce, the subtle bonds of *esprit de corps* and corporate loyalty to dependent subordinates, whom he did not personally know, were not instinctive to him.[281]

Many tributes were paid to Kevin upon his departure from RTÉ and he received many letters of good wishes, including one from the Chief Justice of Hong Kong, which noted:

> I remember once reading an article of how Napolean would have made a success of any role which he had chosen to adopt in life because he had the qualities which are demanded by any exacting task.
>
> It seems that your capacity to meet any challenge has something of the same quality though, fortunately for us you have decided to follow more peaceful vocations.
>
> I imagine that your 5 years with Radio Telefis must have been exacting and exhausting but it must also be very satisfying to have made such a success of so difficult an assignment; one in which you could not possibly please everyone and in which the critics were always likely to be more vocal than the supporters; though I don't think criticism ever worried you unduly.[282]

Tom Hardiman, who succeeded him as Director-General, saw Kevin's greatest contribution in the fact that 'not having been imbued with the sinews and veins of the public service, he gave RTÉ a character, style and presence which would not have been created without him.'[283]

Gay Byrne recalls that in the early days of the new television station, the Government, hierarchy and the establishment in general, were consumed by a 'great urge to control' and that, to his great credit, Kevin, 'with no great instruction book to guide him, set the standards for the future independence of the organisation'.[284]

Perhaps the most fitting tribute was the staff valediction at Kevin's final dinner, delivered by Riobárd O'Farachíain, in which he said:

> I will be fairly brief – if for no other reason than you, Director-General, have no mean flow of words yourself. We have observed this both as one of your managerial accomplishments and as conclusive proof that you are an Irishman – indeed a Kerryman!
>
> You came to us from the business world to which you will shortly return, from the international business world, also from the Irish business world, which you have enriched. We noticed various things: your international and indeed world-wide experience, and the fact that the volcano of the Irish temperament had survived the light frost of the international business experience.
>
> The volcano erupted occasionally and I (and I suppose other colleagues) received allocations or memoranda in which the *ingens fervidum Scotorum* reappeared as it has done since the phrase was coined.
>
> But you were always – or almost always – fair. When you blew us up, so my own experience goes, you never diminished our own authority. When you said to me 'that's a right crowd of (shall I say ladies and gentlemen?) you have in Henry Street', you did add: 'But I gave you authority in my absence and I accept your decision.' This is, in the judgement of an unlearned manager, the quintessence of management.

You entered a complex world as D.G. RTE, and, if I may say so, learned many of our arts *and* crafts very fast.

You have made your mark on broadcasting, and, following as you did many others who shaped it, I think that that is no small tribute.

Another Irish trait – if I may be a little chauvinistic – is your concern for kindly values. You possibly – perhaps probably – met ruthlessness in other phases of your career, but you did not accept it. For this above all I thank you.

The celebrated and intimidating actress, Mrs. Patrick Campbell, once gave a naughty reply to someone who asked her how did she like her new, married state.

She replied: 'Oh, the deep deep peace of the featherbed after the hurly-burly of the chaise-longue'.

I wish you, in your next important post, the peace of the featherbed after the dreadful, hurly-burly of the chaise-longue of broadcasting.[285]

Chapter 6

United Distillers, 1968–78

The 'featherbed' Kevin chose for what was to be his final full-time position was at United Distillers of Ireland, which he joined as Managing Director on 1 April 1968. While its roots could be traced back to the late eighteenth century, United Distillers itself was less than two years old, the result of the merger of Cork Distilleries Co. Ltd, John Jameson & Son Ltd and John Power & Son Ltd in July 1966, after two years of often difficult negotiations.

The three companies were very much family businesses. Cork Distilleries was controlled by the Murphy family, who were direct descendants of James Murphy and his two brothers, the founders of the Midleton Distillery in 1825. The Chairman of John Jameson & Son, Aleck Crichton, was a grandson of a previous chairman, while Frank O'Reilly, Chairman of John Power & Son, was the descendant of James Power, who had founded his distillery in John's Lane, Dublin, in 1791.

The stated objectives of the new merged entity were to make the industry fully competitive in the context of free trade, which was fast approaching, and to create the correct conditions for the expansion of exports. As it stood, the new company dominated the whiskey and gin markets in Ireland. Listed on the Stock Exchange, it had a market capitalisation of almost £8 million, making it the seventh largest industrial concern in Ireland at the time.

Kevin was approached by Frank O'Reilly, who told him that the business was at a crossroads, but there was great potential for an indigenous Irish industry. He was to be the first Managing Director of the new merged entity, on a salary of £12,500 per annum, which one English newspaper suggested was 'one of the highest, if not the highest, salaries paid in Eire'.[286]

Kevin was acutely conscious, from his time at P.J. Carroll's, of the particular challenges faced by a manager in seeking to restructure a business that still had many of the characteristics of a family business. 'I suppose I interviewed them more than they interviewed me,' he recalled. 'I knew something about families in business and here were three of them!'[287]

In the days leading up to his taking charge, Kevin visited all of the company's production and other facilities and met virtually all of the staff. On his first day he invited a number of senior journalists to a 'delightful, standing-up reception' in the Jameson Distillery in Bow Street, a gesture that was very well received, although when one journalist suggested that he must view his new job as 'easy' as he had not met the press for two months after his appointment to RTÉ, Kevin replied that he saw this suggestion as 'slightly daft'.[288] The reception, according to one report, 'was illuminated by Kevin McCourt's almost luminous Indigo suit, worn with a red pocket handkerchief ... as though he was waiting for colour TV.'[289]

The reception proved to be a very good public relations exercise. To the amusement of those present, Kevin declared that while he did not yet know the extent of his advertising budget, none of it would be spent on television. He informed the gathering that the first assault would be on the Northern Ireland market, and the Old Bushmills Distillery in particular, then into England, then four or five Continental countries and, finally, the United States. As one commentator put it the following day: '... With the reputation of being the super salesman of our time, Kevin McCourt now has the job of selling Powers, Jameson and the CDC Group, and all their works and pomps, and of putting these Irish Distilleries into the top line ranked names in exports.'[290]

Kevin decided to set up headquarters in Bow Street, so that he could 'live with the highly skilled men who make what he is selling.'[291] To underline the point, he arranged that the offices in St Stephen's Green, which had been leased before his arrival as a 'neutral' headquarters, were rented to someone else the day before he took up his appointment.

On 9 April 1968, nine days into the job, Kevin issued his first report to the board as Managing Director. In it he highlighted the fact that there was a scarcity of people of calibre in group management and that he required senior appointments in both marketing and personnel. He sought approval for the immediate appointment of Clem Ryan as Group Production Director. This early appointment would prove hugely significant for the company. Ryan, a member of the family that had owned Powers, had argued for the modernisation of the distilling facilities both to achieve efficiencies and to facilitate the development of a new refined whiskey product.

While significantly growing the export side of the business was the number one priority, a rationalisation of the group's production facilities—the Jameson Distillery in Bow Street and the John Power Distillery in John's Lane, both in Dublin, and former CDC operations in Cork City and in Midleton—was also required. The Jameson and Power Distilleries in Dublin were constrained by the growth of the city around them, leaving no room for expansion. In addition, the physical separation of the distilleries in Dublin and Cork posed significant challenges to effective integration. The absence of production rationalisation had prevented the merged company gaining any real economy of scale. Its profits for its first full year to 30 September 1967, at just over £600,000 pre-tax, were lower than the aggregate of the profits of the three separate companies in the previous year. While exports grew in the year to September 1968, the excessive cost base meant that pre-tax profit for that year was even lower at just over £520,000, with net profit just £284,000.

Speaking at the Annual General Meeting of the company in February 1969, the Chairman, Frank O'Reilly, noted that 'rising costs are a source of great anxiety to your Board' and that the board intended to 'attack all cost centres as expeditiously as possible', particularly as time was against them with free trade with Great Britain 'around the corner'.[292]

Kevin had already begun the task of reorganising the business, unifying marketing and sales on a group-wide basis and creating four main divisions catering for Production, Finance, Marketing and Research & Development. The establishment of a new, unified management team was far from an easy task, however. While the formal merger had occurred in June 1966, operational integration had barely begun. As Kevin found on his arrival, there was no personnel function. The family companies had been, both metaphorically and literally, paternalistic. Kevin chose as Director of Personnel Ronnie Robinson, who had previously been a director of John Jameson. By choosing Robinson he hoped to maintain some of the old firms' traditional associations. 'Personnel is a very complex area in a business as old as this,' he once pointed out.[293] While senior appointments such as Clem Ryan (Production), Aleck Crichton (Research & Development) and David Dillon (Finance) came from within, Kevin did not hesitate to look outside, most notably in the appointment of Archie Cook as Marketing Director. 'What I'm trying to do is to build up professional management,' Kevin pointedly explained. 'I think the day of the good all-rounder, whether he comes from a distinguished family or not, is over.'[294]

Any benefits that might have been thought to accrue in the early months of the new financial year were at risk of being offset by a three-week nationwide strike by maintenance workers. According to Frank O'Reilly at the AGM, this had not only nullified increased domestic sales because deliveries had become impossible but had also hit at exports, with 17,000 cases for twenty-one countries awaiting shipment indefinitely. Three days later, writing in *Business and Finance* magazine, Kevin declared that the uncertainty in labour relations had made it 'a bad start to a year which should be used to add well-being to the national economic progress of last year' and that 'without some predictability ... in relations with employees at all levels, corporate planning is aborted.'[295]

To assist in the rationalisation programme, Kevin retained the services of the US management consultants Arthur D. Little, on the stated basis that he had 'a feel for the American approach'.[296] While their advice would no doubt prove valuable, there was also a sense that the potentially sensitive verdict on which distilleries were to be closed might be delivered more easily by Americans. After six months' work the company was in a position to announce its plans. At a press conference held on 22 August 1969, it was announced that the four production facilities would be consolidated into a single, large, modern facility that, subject to further study, would take the form of a major extension and complete modernisation of the distillery at Midleton, County Cork, where the company owned a 48-acre site. As a first step, Dublin production was to be centralised in the John's Lane plant, with the overall consolidation expected to take up to five years. Kevin confirmed that redundancies arising from the immediate Dublin consolidation would be confined to seasonal part-time workers and that no permanent employees would be affected by the moves 'for some years'.[297] He indicated that the likely cost of developing the new facility was upwards of £1 million.

The financial results for the year to September 1969 showed 'a sparkling recovery in trading performance'.[298] Pre-tax profits had jumped by 50 per cent to almost £830,000 on the back of substantial increases in both home and export markets and reflecting the results of the first significant rationalisation moves. A significant contribution was also made by Edward Dillon & Co., a wine and spirit merchant in which the company had taken a 65 per cent majority interest in May of that year.

The results were received enthusiastically by the market and the business media. 'Mighty recovery for United Distillers', 'UDI exceed expectations with record performance' and 'UDI sparkles on investor confidence'[299] were among the gratifying headlines. Most of the plaudits were given to Kevin, since it had not gone unnoticed that the record performance coincided with his first full year as Managing Director.

The key initiative Kevin took in relation to the domestic market was the decision to deal directly with retailers. Unsurprisingly, it was a decision that generated considerable anger among the wholesalers, who had dealt with the company and its predecessor companies for many years. In reality, wholesalers had enjoyed generous credit terms with domestic distillers, which had frequently been used to subsidise their imports businesses.

If Kevin's ambition of significant direct sales to the retail trade was to be achieved, the major obstacle of the timing of payment of Government duty—by far the largest element in the price of spirits—needed to be addressed. Duty was payable on product before it could be released from bond. Kevin was conscious, again from his time at P.J. Carroll's, of the negative effects of a similar duty regime.

With the help of Gene Savage and David Dillon, Kevin succeeded in persuading the Government to allow a period of six weeks for deferred payment of duty, which would roughly equate to the credit terms traditionally enjoyed by the retail trade from wholesalers. Since the Government required duty arising in any particular fiscal year to be paid in that year, an arrangement was reached whereby coming up to the end of the year, duty was paid on a daily basis. The new duty arrangements allowed the company to deal with retailers on terms attractive to both sides and had a dramatic impact on the company's working capital.

With rationalisation plans underway, the domestic market altered radically by the introduction of direct sales to retailers and shareholders mollified, at least for the present, Kevin's focus turned to export markets. The company faced an unprotected home market at the start of 1971, with the result that Scotch could soon be sold at the same price as Irish whiskey. The benefit the company had derived from the protection of duties was evidenced by the fact that the Scotch share of the Irish market had fallen from 21 per cent in the 1950s to 13 per cent by the end of the 1960s. Faced with this challenge the company sought new horizons and, in particular, in the biggest market of all: the United States.

First up, however, was the announcement that Reggie O'Reilly, who had been moved from his position as Sales and Marketing Manager at Powers to the role of Export Manager of the group, was to travel to Japan for the opening of Expo '70 in Osaka, where United Distillers was the only Irish private enterprise company exhibiting in the Irish Pavilion. Expo '70, which was to run for six months, was expected to draw large numbers of businessmen and tourists, and the company's decision to participate was a clear signal of intent in relation to its global ambitions. Later, Kevin would develop close links with the Japanese brewing company Suntory.

Kevin was under no illusion about how difficult it might prove to make a significant breakthrough in the US market. Before the First World War, Irish whiskey had been the principal imported spirit in the US, with almost 400 brands available. But civil strife and economic depression caused a number of distilleries in Ireland to close; barley malt was in short supply because most of the grain was needed for food. Government restrictions aimed at keeping excise money flowing at home reduced exports of whiskey to a trickle; the restrictions were not lifted until 1952. In the US, sales of Irish whiskey fell badly as imported Scotch filled the demand. In 1969, even allowing for an impressive 10 per cent increase in sales, 110,000 cases of Irish whiskey had been sold in the US compared with 15 million cases of Scotch.

While the need to crack the US market was compelling, Kevin was conscious that 'change in this industry tends to come in decades, not in months, and the long maturation of our product after it has been created means that what the production function is doing now greatly influences what the marketing function will be doing in up to ten years' time.'[300] 'Shortly after we enter the 70s,' he wrote, 'this company will have to start planning for the 80s.'[301]

In Kevin's view, the assault on the US market had three requisites: meticulous planning, ensuring the product was right and an aggressive marketing campaign. Kevin had long believed in formalised corporate planning as essential to identifying and achieving a business' long-term objectives, and that such planning should be continually brought up-to-date as circumstances changed. Writing in December 1969, he explained: 'We aim to create the corporate objectives far enough ahead so that the production and marketing function, the two key elements of a business, are formalised into a total plan.'[302]

After ensuring the corporate plan was in place, attention now focussed on the suitability of Irish whiskey for the US market. Kevin was clear that 'consumer taste may be influenced, but it cannot be bludgeoned.'[303] The reality was that consumer whiskey tastes had been swinging for some time towards lighter or less flavoured offerings. To many Americans, Irish whiskey was a 'rough, heavy liquor with a spit and sawdust image'.[304] Kevin quoted one American distributor as saying, 'Take the boxing gloves out of your whiskey and I'll be able to sell it.'[305]

Scotch producers had already launched a highly successful lighter product in the US and US bourbon producers were planning to do likewise. By January 1970, Kevin was able to announce that the spearhead of the onslaught into the US would be a 'modified' Jameson, which would be test-marketed in America in April or May. 'We haven't invented a Scotch and we haven't invented a bourbon,' Kevin declared, 'we've tailored an Irish whiskey to suit a light taste market.'[306]

The US campaign was to be based not only on the new lighter Jameson but was also to feature the group's other principal brands, Tullamore Dew, Power's and Paddy. A major US public relations agency, Edward Gottlieb and Associates, was retained to advise on a three-year campaign and to work with the advertising agencies already on board for the individual US importers handling the company's brands. Leaving nothing to chance, Crossley Surveys were retained to produce taste-test results and Ernest Dichter were commissioned to carry out a motivational study. The bar was set extraordinarily high: to grow by 30 per cent year on year over as many as ten years.

In an interview in July 1970, Reggie O'Reilly stated that the campaign would project not only new aspects of Irish whiskey but of Ireland itself. He admitted that the company remained haunted by stereotypes drawn from Irish immigrant days, which cast some doubt on marketing images and brand symbolism, but he was optimistic, citing the acceptance of new Canadian brands in the US as a good sign. He also mysteriously announced that later in the year the company would introduce a whiskey ambassadress to the US—in O'Reilly's words, 'a red-haired surprise'.[307]

In November, all was revealed. Months of preparatory work were to culminate in a visit to the US by Kevin, where he would address the twenty-first Annual Convention of the National Licensed Beverage Association in New Jersey. The event would be attended by over 2,000 delegates and Kevin would become the first Irishman invited to address the Convention. Kevin's visit was to coincide with the end of a six-week promotional tour of the US and Canada by the Irish ambassadress, who was revealed to be Kathleen Watkins. Kathleen was a renowned singer and musician, with considerable experience in Ireland on both radio and television. She was also the wife of the broadcaster, Gay Byrne. Her role was to describe the modern Irish way of life on television, radio and in special addresses, wearing outfits specially designed by the leading Irish couturiers of the day.

The initial campaign in the US proved to be of limited success. United Distillers was a very minor player in a highly competitive and developed market. What was of enormous significance, however, was the development of a new style of whiskey—the Jameson North American Blend, which was pioneered by Clem Ryan and his production team and supported enthusiastically by Kevin. It would prove to be the building-block from which Jameson would develop in the coming decades as one of the world's fastest-growing and most durable brands. Critically, agreement was reached with the Revenue Commissioners that the new blend was a new product, thus qualifying for export sales relief.

The results for the year to September 1970 represented a further milestone, with pre-tax profits passing £1 million, up 43 per cent on the previous year. The figures were announced while Kevin was in the US, prompting a telegram from Archie Cook and Reggie O'Reilly: 'Delighted. News. Congratulations. Busy heading for second million!'[308]

While the year 1970 may be recalled as the year in which United Distillers launched its export drive into the US, it could have been witness to a much more dramatic development. On 29 April 1970 the Investment Bank of Ireland (IBI) issued a press release to the effect that four major Irish businesses—Waterford Glass, P.J. Carroll, The Irish Glass Bottle Company and United Distillers—were in discussion to examine means by which they could form a strong Irish industrial group. Each company would continue its separate trading identity but, the press release continued:

> ... the combination of their human and financial resources will strengthen the ability of each to compete successfully in export markets throughout the world to the benefit of employees, shareholders and the national economy as a whole.

The press release set out the backdrop to the discussions:

> The Anglo-Irish Free Trade Agreement and possibly in due course full membership of the European Economic Community will present Irish industry with very considerable opportunities, but will also expose it to intense

competition. Full advantage can best be taken of these opportunities by developing existing management ability and techniques to the highest standard, coupled with substantial capital resources. Such a group would be better placed to meet competition that is already operating on a multi-national basis than would the individual companies acting alone.[309]

Messrs. Cooper Brothers & Co., Chartered Accountants, were retained to assist in submitting detailed proposals for consideration by the boards of each of the companies and, in due course, by their shareholders.

The announcement, as the *Irish Press* reported on the following day, 'created quite a furore in business circles but after getting over the initial shock, most people greeted it very enthusiastically.'[312] One Dublin financier was quoted as saying: 'I can just picture myself drinking some UDI whiskey poured from an IGB bottle into a Waterford crystal glass, while smoking a High King.'[311]

One of the most striking features of the proposed merger was the number of cross-over relations at board level, most obviously in relation to the board of the principal advisor, IBI, which included John A. Ryan (also a director of United Distillers), Don Carroll (Chairman of P.J. Carroll and a director of United Distillers) and Patrick McGrath (Chairman of both Waterford Glass and Irish Glass Bottle). Waterford Glass shared five directors in common with its one-time parent, Irish Glass Bottle.

The rationale for the move was generally viewed as marketing, with a clear emphasis on export development. In this context United Distillers and P.J. Carroll were seen as having a significant opportunity to benefit from the marketing skills so evident in Waterford Glass' success, particularly in the US market. A major impediment to the merger was the outstanding performance by Waterford Glass, which was reflected in a market capitalisation of six times its net asset worth. A distribution based on market capitalisation would have entitled Waterford Glass shareholders to 48 per cent of the equity of the new conglomerate, which was unlikely to find favour with the shareholders in the other companies. Another perceived difficulty was the scattered nature of the United Distillers shareholding, with doubts as to whether the old John Power shareholders, in particular, would be enthusiastic about a second merger in four years.

There was also inevitable speculation as to who might end up running the new merged entity. The companies themselves maintained a complete silence on this and every aspect of the discussions. The fact that Kevin was in a unique position, having run two of the four entities, made him a likely candidate.

Kevin was strongly opposed to the merger, arguing forcibly that there was no hard evidence that real synergies could be achieved and that there was greater potential for United Distillers' shareholders if the company remained independent. While Coopers Brothers prepared joint sets of figures for the four entities, Kevin initiated a detailed internal review to support the argument for independence. To assist him he obtained the services, on secondment from Peat Marwick Mitchell in London, of a young Irish accountant, Richard Burrows. Burrows had worked on the audit of United Distillers and had spent a previous stint on secondment with the company. He recalled:

> Kevin whistled me back from London to work on a defence strategy, which meant building a long-term plan for Irish Distillers – on that basis the board would be enabled to take a view as to whether or not the merger made sense. I worked on the strategy for five or six months and, the

more I worked on it, the more obvious it became that for Irish Distillers this was going to be disastrous.[312]

The merger discussions ended without agreement. A statement from IBI in January 1971 confirmed that the boards of the companies had concluded that 'the benefits likely to flow from an association are not sufficiently concrete to warrant further study'.[313]

In addition to the new blend of whiskey targeting the US market, 1970 and 1971 saw the introduction into the product range of Huzzar Vodka, Kiskadee White Rum and Commodore Gin, to complement Cork Dry Gin. Following the success of the new whiskey in the US, a new lighter blend for the home market, Midleton Reserve, was developed. *The Sunday Times* declared:

> Only a Scot would have the nerve to interfere with an Irishman's favourite whiskey and Archie Cook has done it twice, which would normally qualify him for a quick crack with a blunt shillelagh.[314]

A decision was also taken to change the name of the group to Irish Distillers Group (IDG).

In September 1971, Kevin was invited by the editor of the *Sunday Independent* to contribute four articles on any current business issues of his choosing. Other leading business people were invited to do likewise. On Sunday 7 November the first of Kevin's articles was published. It was on the broad theme of the imperative of buying Irish-manufactured goods:

> I can see no reason why there should be a predilection to prefer the importation simply because its foreignness gives it some imaginary cachet - especially when local equivalents, equally good or better and equally keenly priced, are available. This is not only nonsense but dangerous

nonsense which attacks the roots of our national prosperity.[315]

Kevin's second article, examining the complexities facing the Irish exporter, was due for publication the following Sunday. The National Union of Journalists cried foul. While they did not object to Kevin, or any other non-journalist, having one article published, they could not agree to such people being allowed to publish a series of articles. Management refused to back down, leading to the NUJ blacking publication of the *Evening Herald* on Saturday 13 November and also of the *Sunday Independent* on 14 November. The dispute spread to the other newspapers, with the result that on Monday 15 November the *Irish Independent, Irish Press* and *The Irish Times* were not published. At this stage Kevin intervened, withdrew his second article and announced that he would not contribute the remaining two articles.

In addition to his commitments at Irish Distillers and as a non-executive director on various boards, Kevin was an active member of the Confederation of Irish Industry, the successor to his former employer, the Federation of Irish Manufacturers. In 1972 the Confederation, like all business organisations, was focussed on the implications for Irish business to accession of the European Economic Community (EEC).

On 18 June 1972 twelve leaders of Irish industry lost their lives in an air crash at Staines, in London, while on their way to Brussels for discussions on accession. These included the President (Con Smith) and Director General (E.J. Gray) of the Confederation, the Director of the Irish Council of the European Movement, Michael Sweetman, the Chairman of the Irish Employers' Confederation, Ivan Webb, and the President of the Dublin Chamber of Commerce, Michael O'Reilly. The visit by the businessmen had been arranged on two previous occasions, but had been postponed due to the unavailability of relevant people in Brussels. Kevin was a member of the delegation and was booked to travel on each of the two earlier occasions. He had reluctantly withdrawn from the trip on 18 June because he was returning from the United States on the previous day.

The Staines crash had an enormous impact on the Irish business community and it greatly affected Kevin. A number of those who died were very close friends of his. As he wrote three days after the tragedy: 'The loss of these men is a hard blow to Ireland – we just do not have many people of this calibre.'[316]

The merger of the three Irish distilling companies in 1966 had created from the outset the potential that the new entity would become a takeover target. One of the attractions of the four-way merger talks in 1970 was that the resulting conglomerate could well have served as a protection from unwelcome external advances for each of its components. The imperative for Irish Distillers to increase exports—and the not inconsiderable barriers to achieving that growth by acting alone—led Kevin to consider options for co-operating with major foreign drinks companies. In September 1972 Frank O'Reilly found it necessary to reject rumours that Joseph Seagrams & Sons, the largest distilling group in the world, had approached Irish Distillers with a view to making a takeover offer.

While Frank O'Reilly's statement was technically correct at the time it was made, there had been a number of discussions, going back to October 1971, between Kevin and the then President of the US division of Seagrams, Jack Yogman, who had been touring the world seeking out investment opportunities. When his initial approach was rebuffed by the IDG Board,

Yogman, with Kevin's encouragement, decided to look elsewhere on the island.

The Old Bushmills Distillery in County Antrim was owned by Bass Charrington. Kevin would have dearly loved to acquire Old Bushmills for IDG, but political and religious sensitivities made this virtually impossible. Things were different for an American company, however, and in January 1972 Yogman telephoned Kevin to inform him that he had agreed, in principle, with Bass Charrington that they would sell Old Bushmills to Seagrams. Following discussions with the IDG Board, Kevin replied that Yogman should not assume that IDG would wish to acquire it from Seagrams or have Seagrams acquire part of IDG's equity.

Discussions continued throughout most of 1972. Eventually, in October, Seagrams announced publicly that it had acquired Old Bushmills. At the same time, Seagrams also announced that having bought the County Antrim distillery for £4 million, it had agreed to sell a 25 per cent stake in it to Irish Distillers for £1 million and had agreed to acquire a 15 per cent stake in Irish Distillers for £3.35 million, a figure that represented a very significant premium to the market price of IDG shares at the time. 'It was a measure of how badly they wanted in,' Kevin recalled. 'It was the best deal I ever did.'[317]

The net effect of the Seagrams deal for IDG was a cash injection of £2.35 million and an important strategic stake in the only other significant distillery in Ireland—a distillery that could claim to be the oldest distillery in the world, with thirteenth-century origins, and that had been licensed to distil since 1608, which predated the Scotch distillers' licenses. Of greater contemporary relevance, however, was the fact that it also distilled the most successful Irish whiskey exported to the US market. Seagrams was represented on the IDG board by Charles Bronfman.

Although the deal with Seagrams was approved at a

shareholders' meeting of IDG in November 1972, some questions were raised in relation to the rationale for the deal. In his statement announcing the deal, Frank O'Reilly focussed on the increased export potential, asserting that IDG had 'acquired additional resources, outlets and promotional support in major export markets, which could not so readily have been attained by our own individual efforts'.[318] For others, it was viewed as a defensive move. Seagrams had agreed not to make a takeover bid and its stake could serve as an important block to anyone else's ambitions in this regard. Two potentially interested acquirers were identified as Waterford Glass and Fitzwilton. One commentator suggested, in that context, that part of the rationale for the Seagrams deal was that 'Kevin McCourt would undoubtedly not be too keen to play second fiddle to Noel Griffin or Tony O'Reilly'.[319] Whatever the interest from Waterford Glass, the fact that Fitzwilton, and in particular O'Reilly, kept a keen eye on IDG was borne out a decade-and-a-half later when they unsuccessfully made an approach to IDG on becoming aware that Seagrams was proposing to sell its stake.

The relationship with Seagrams brought benefits to IDG, not least in giving the company access to significant technical expertise. There was a sense, however, from the start, that the relationship could not achieve its full potential. Seagrams' original ambition had been to own a larger, perhaps even a majority, stake in IDG. The insistence of the board that Seagrams commit to maintaining a minority role inevitably led to Seagrams' commitment being less than it might have been. It also meant that Seagrams would one day be likely to seek to realise its investment. When it eventually decided to do so, IDG would become the subject of a bitter takeover battle—the very thing the board had hoped could be avoided in reaching the original deal with Seagrams.

Seagrams' contribution to IDG's efforts to crack the crucial US market—the market that Kevin viewed as 'Irish Distiller's Klondike', in Richard Burrows' words[320]—also failed to live up to Kevin's expectations. Seagrams was the sole importer of Jameson in the United States, with Brown Forman importing Bushmills. Sales growth in both products proved disappointing, certainly relative to the effort and investment made.

In April 1974 IDG gained control of Old Bushmills by acquiring a further 55 per cent of its shares, in return for which Seagrams' shareholding in IDG increased to 20 per cent, although Seagrams undertook to retain its voting strength at 15 per cent.

It was inevitable that, at a time when tensions in Northern Ireland were running very high, a company based in the Republic of Ireland gaining control of a centuries-old County Antrim business would give rise to some considerable local concern. Kevin met with local management and trade unions to explain, in person, the plans for further development of the Old Bushmills plant. He also made a point of meeting the local Member of Parliament, the Reverend Ian Paisley. At their meeting, Paisley recalled how Kevin had shown him considerable courtesy a few years earlier when, as Director-General of RTÉ, he had welcomed Paisley on one of his rare visits south. This made the Bushmills meeting a lot less difficult than might have been anticipated, with Kevin persuading Paisley that the acquisition of a majority stake in Old Bushmills was in the long-term interest of his constituents.[321]

The acquisition of a majority stake in Old Bushmills made eminent business sense, although there was some media criticism that IDG had paid a price proportionally the same as that which it paid for its first stake, even though Old Bushmills' profits were considerably lower than originally anticipated.

Eventually, in January 1978, IDG bought Seagrams' remaining 20 per cent in Old Bushmills for £1.2 million, paid in cash.

By late 1974 Kevin could look back on his first six and a half years in charge at IDG with some pride. A new management structure installed, a fresh corporate culture created, a successful rationalisation programme implemented, the beginnings of export growth, an alliance with Seagrams, a majority stake in Old Bushmills, a state-of-the-art distillery set to open and increasing profitability year on year all added up to a very creditable performance. But in November 1974 much of this progress was put in jeopardy when the company was hit by an all-out strike. The cause of the strike was not, as might have been feared, concerns over job security in the context of the planned opening at Midleton and the closure of the other facilities, but rather an argument over pay differentials between craftsmen and general workers. It lasted fourteen weeks, during which all of the company's facilities in the Republic of Ireland were closed. The strike hit the peak Christmas period, and was not resolved until February 1975. The results for the half-year to March 1975 showed profits at a mere £64,000, and although sales recovered in the second half of the year, profits for the year to September 1975 fell by 63 per cent to under £1 million. Writing at the end of 1974, at the height of the strike, Kevin declared:

> Simplest of all in expression, if not in performance, is the need for more work. Our country is involved in a war, a war about standards of living, a war that threatens the development we all legitimately seek. Were it a shooting war, we would all be working very hard not to be killed.
>
> We can go a long way towards winning our share in Ireland of this particular war by putting in more than we

try to take out, by some reduction in self-interest in favour of the national well-being.[322]

While IDG and its predecessor companies had experienced strikes in the past, none had been on this scale nor had continued for this length of time. For a consumer-facing business so reliant on having its products available at all times for its customers, the strike undoubtedly weakened the company's hold on the domestic market. That the strike was ultimately settled on the terms the unions had sought initially made the episode appear all the more futile.

Speaking to the Company's management conference in October 1977, Kevin recalled:

> We had the calamity of a fourteen weeks' strike with tremendously serious consequences for Irish Distillers Ltd and the cause for most profound thinking and lesson-learning by all of us responsible for managing our business. Friends of mine in the Trade Union movement at the time told me that a strike is inevitable in every company from time to time and that when it occurs, one must just put up with it until lessons have been learned on both sides and everybody gets back to work again. I caution that we must never assume that a strike is inevitable and that we will have another one some time or another. There are circumstances sometimes we do not control during which a situation gallops away from us, but I believe now out of the deep pain and distress which that strike of ours caused we must always be anticipating the relationships between people who work in the company, never dismissing the smallest measure of conflict as being inconsequential and always trying to have communion with those who like ourselves work in the company but who do not always have

the same measure of understanding or the same access to information and who themselves may come under external pressure which would promote a we and they relationship. No strike is a good strike and no company today will benefit from a strike.[323]

In an interview to mark his retirement in 1978, Kevin described that strike as one 'which needn't have happened, that leaves a scar on my back'.[324]

The poor results to September 1975 and a less-than-promising start to the new financial year led to a new experience for the Board of IDG: a critical and at times stormy AGM in February 1976. Frank O'Reilly came under fire from some shareholders on the perceived slippage by Irish whiskey against Scotch in the domestic market, but more forcefully in relation to the relationship with Seagrams and the failure of the Board to disclose US sales figures. At the meeting, Jack Yogman sought to defend Seagrams' efforts in the US on behalf of IDG. Within a few months he would be forced to resign his position as worldwide President of Seagrams as earnings in the Seagrams Group declined.

In the meantime, production at the new IDG Midleton plant commenced in December 1975. The cost of the development was over £7 million—a multiple of the original estimate. It was the first new distillery opened in Ireland in more than a century and one of the most modern in the world.

It took some time for the company to recover from the difficulties caused by the strike, but by September 1977 the benefits of concentrating production at Midleton and a significant growth in exports saw pre-tax profits rise to almost £3.4 million. By then Kevin had announced his intention to retire as Managing Director. It was announced that Richard

Burrows—who had been appointed by Seagrams as Managing Director of Bushmills six years earlier, at the age of twenty-six, and who was later appointed by Kevin as General Manager of IDG—was to replace him.

Kevin explained his decision to his management colleagues in the following terms:

> Nobody said I must retire. Indeed, I had to ask them to release me from contract. I am not bored, I am not ill, I am not retiring to start another career. I am retiring because I believe it is the right thing to do at this stage of the company's strength – when it is successful – on a launching pad to far greater successes, rejuvenated by new and younger management.[325]

In an interview with the publication *Management*, he elaborated on the reasons behind his decision:

> It is a good time to have a good look at myself and ask myself what I really want to do. I have not been able to have much family life. My family have all grown up and gone off and done their own things and thank God for that. But I owe something to Peggy, my wife, and I might indulge myself a bit and say I owe something to myself, to share a bit more with her, to see a bit more of my children.[326]

In his address to the AGM in February 1978, Frank O'Reilly paid generous tribute to Kevin, who he said had made a 'truly remarkable contribution to Irish Distillers during what has been a relatively short period of time'. Kevin, for his part, wrote to O'Reilly:

> We had a tremendous ten years together, and any differences were as nothing by comparison with our

understanding of the objectives and knowing the difficulties and the personality problems to be handled, to be firm about, or to be won over.

It is well-known, because I frequently have said it, that I would not have joined the group in 1967 had it not been dealing with you as Chairman and person. Looking back at it all, I think now that the arrangements we made at that time were the easiest, the quickest, and in the long run, the most satisfactory and least contentious of all the innumerable negotiations and contracts and battles that followed in the next ten years.

We had a great understanding about people and situations and about what was right or wrong in different circumstances, even if it was sometimes instinct, commonsense or just plain decency that motivated us rather than analysis and pragmatism. We were complementary to each other in our instincts and in our confidence about what we could make of our Company.

So, Frank, you share in a major way in whatever I did in the last ten years; you rendered more safe and passable for me the more dangerous and difficult paths which my impetuosity and short-sightedness would otherwise have turned into plain jungle.[327]

Kevin retired from IDG on 31 March 1978—'ten years to the day I joined', as he recorded as his last entry in his IDG diary. *The Irish Times* of that day noted:

> When Kevin C. McCourt hands over his metaphorical corkscrew as managing director of Irish Distillers Group tonight it will mark the end of the first phase of the most revolutionary period in the history of that ancient and highly traditional industry.

> In the 10 years that he was at the helm in Bow Street, McCourt not only modified and modernised the traditional (and very individual) product to meet the tastes of the rising generation; he also masterminded the amalgamation of the highly individualised firms of the group into a single modern distillery on the site of the old Midleton house, and he brought in Old Bushmills from the North, thus establishing a single block of all Ireland distillers.
>
> McCourt is almost passionately Irish in the best sense of that term, which is to say that he has a proper pride in his heritage and faith in the potential of this country without any trace of chauvinism. It would be hard for anybody who has travelled as widely through the world as he has to be narrowly chauvinistic or to have other than a clean-cut perspective about this country.[328]

Years later, his colleague, Ted Bonner, admittedly a man not renowned for under-statement, referred to Kevin's time at IDG as a 'brilliant tenure—a period in which he virtually brought about a renaissance of the entire industry'.[329]

At the time of his retirement, Kevin summed up the achievements at IDG during his tenure as Managing Director:

> We have rationalised – which was the intent of the whole thing. Our business has grown very substantially. We have made great progress in overseas markets and are still growing there. We have adapted our products to suit tastes overseas, something that the individual distillers would never have done for fear of making the mistake of being a one-off. We also took the traumatic decision to close down the traditional family distillers. These were hard decisions. They were associated for several generations with those distillers but they made the sensible and logical decision.

I suppose they were made easier by having an independent, emotionally removed chief executive.[330]

The United Distillers Kevin had joined in 1968 was an amalgamation of three proud, traditional family companies whose owners took a bold step in acknowledging that the Irish distilling industry could best survive and prosper if their companies merged, but who, having done so, struggled with what to do next. It is to their credit that they saw the need for professional management from outside and that they chose, in Kevin, a manager noted for his directness and independence, one who was 'emotionally removed' from the history of the distilleries. Kevin brought optimism, direction, determination and a freshness of approach. In doing so, he was the catalyst that allowed the families to achieve for their businesses a place on the distilling world stage—the goal of which they had long dreamed. By deconstructing the notion of the family firm, Kevin helped preserve the business—unlike what happened at the British Distillers Company, which pandered to the whims of the individual proprietors for decades and reaped the reward of extinction. The new blend of Jameson whiskey developed under his guidance, the acquisition of Old Bushmills, the oldest operating distillery in the world, and the development of the most modern distillery facility in the world at Midleton were all monuments to his time at IDG.

Chapter 7

Irish Steel, 1974–86

In December 1974 Justin Keating, the Minister for Industry and Commerce, appointed Kevin Chairman of the State-sponsored Irish Steel Holdings Ltd (ISH). In 1965 Kevin had appointed Keating as Editor of agricultural programmes at RTÉ, which had proved a controversial appointment, not least because of objections from some quarters that Keating was a veterinary, rather than an agricultural science, graduate. He was also known to hold left-wing views. At a meeting of the RTÉ Authority, one member referred to allegations that Keating was a communist. Kevin strongly defended his choice, asserting that the political or religious convictions of a member of the staff should not enter into the reckoning of suitability for appointment, a view accepted by the Authority, which endorsed the appointment.[331]

Keating was aware that the existing Irish Steel mill was not viable in the long term. He was also very conscious of the need to protect, as far as possible, the livelihoods of the hundreds of men who worked there. For the position of Chairman, he wanted someone with vigour and international business experience, and he immediately thought of Kevin. For his part, Kevin was under no illusion that the role being offered to him had the capacity to become a poisoned chalice. Keating recalls Kevin's 'rueful smile' on accepting the position.[332]

Even at that time, neither the Minister nor Kevin could have predicted the extent of the major storms that were brewing for the international steel industry. Certainly neither could have envisaged that what was intended as a four-year non-executive role—Kevin was still Managing Director of Irish Distillers at the time—would develop into a major eleven-year challenge.

The company had been formed in 1947 on the initiative of Seán Lemass, notwithstanding trenchant opposition from the Department of Finance,[333] and had acquired the assets of the Irish Steel business at Haulbowline, in County Cork, from the receiver appointed to that company. It was the second occasion on which a receiver had been appointed since the business began in 1939. Since 1942 the business had been controlled, in practical terms, by the Government, with the Minister for Finance providing a guarantee of the loan financing the business and the Minister for Industry and Commerce appointing the members of the board.

During the General Election campaign of 1948 opposition spokesmen, who would become Ministers in the Inter-Party Government formed after that election, characterised the steel industry as one of the 'white elephants' Lemass had created at public expense and risk and recommended that it should be abandoned. As with Lemass' subsequent attitude towards the Inter-Party Government's IDA initiative, the threat to reverse the decision to have the State directly involved in the steel industry was quietly abandoned.

The trading history of ISH between 1947 and Kevin's appointment as Chairman at the end of 1974 had been turbulent at times. The business had been relatively successful in the late 1960s and early 1970s, helped by an increased global demand for steel products. In the financial year to June 1974 the company had achieved record net profits of £846,000, and yet at the AGM held in December the outgoing Chairman, G.P.S. Hogan, who had been on the board since the company's beginnings in 1947, sounded a note of caution and predicted reduced turnover and profits in the forthcoming year.[334] Sadly for the company, and for Kevin in his first year as Chairman, this would prove to be a gross understatement.

The company had recognised for a long time that the accession of Ireland to membership of the EEC in January 1973 could have a profound effect on its business. As early as 1957, when the six countries that had formed the European Coal and Steel Community (ECSC) in 1951 formed the EEC, ISH had formally notified the Department of Industry and Commerce that it would be unable to meet free competition as envisaged by the Treaty of Paris. When, in 1963, the Government applied for full membership of the Community, the company instigated efforts—which continued right up to accession a decade later—to find an appropriate external partner to protect the Irish steel industry from the hazards of being required to compete, on equal terms, with the powerful producers in the larger Community countries. Although those efforts proved futile, ISH expressed itself satisfied with concessions secured for it by the Government as part of the accession negotiations.

The challenges posed by accession to the EEC were, in fact, to prove of secondary importance. The year 1975 witnessed a worldwide collapse in demand in the steel market, the like of which had not been experienced for forty years. In the EEC, steel plants were running at barely 60 per cent capacity and were selling product at around 50 per cent of cost. It was estimated that British Steel was losing £5 million a week. In the financial year to June 1975, the turnover of ISH fell by 23 per cent, with the result that the net profit of over £840,000 in the previous year was replaced by a net loss of over £680,000. At the company's AGM, Kevin characterised the outlook for the following year as 'extremely bleak'. As well as a dramatic drop in demand, ISH had to contend with offers of foreign steel at ridiculously low prices. Kevin vented his annoyance at what he saw as the ineffective response of the European Commission:

> In almost every case, the quoted price was either in contravention of the Community price rules, or was insufficient to cover even direct costs of production … Despite strong and virtually unanimous pressure by European steel producers, including your company, the Commission in Brussels has so far failed to take, what we would regard as decisive steps to cope with this, admittedly complex, situation.[335]

The dramatic change in the fortunes of the company and the realisation that global events would likely mean that the business would continue to trade at a loss for the foreseeable future required the company to take urgent action. A decision was taken to suspend production from the electric arc furnace as a temporary measure. A voluntary redundancy scheme was introduced. As a result of this scheme, the laying-off of temporary and casual workers and the non-filling of vacancies, the ISH workforce reduced from over 1,100 in 1974 to just over 700 two years later. As expected, however, the financial results to June 1976 saw further losses of over £1.3 million—twice the level of losses recorded in 1975. 'The years 1975 and 1976 would rank with the blackest ever in the history of the world steel industry,' Kevin declared in his report to the AGM.[336]

For a number of years ISH had been working on a development plan predicated on external involvement. In October 1975 the board informed the Minister that it had retained the services of a Canadian consultancy firm, Ferrco—whose

Chairman was a colourful character of Irish descent, Gerry Heffernan—to develop a plan on a 'go it alone' basis. A detailed plan was submitted to the Government in 1976. In February 1977 the Government announced its support for the proposals.

'Gigantic not only in its cost but in its concept,' was how Kevin described the plan approved by the Government.[337]

It envisaged a significant upgrading in production facilities, including a new 90-tonne furnace, with three times the capacity of the existing furnace, to cater for a more than doubling of production capacity, with more than half of the finished products to be sold in export markets. The estimated cost of the plan was £40 million, including £11.5 million for working capital. The cost was to be funded by way of an equity subscription from the Government of £6 million, an IDA grant of £4 million and borrowings of £30 million. Assuming export targets were reached, there would be a net gain of £10 million per annum to the country's balance of payments. Kevin held a press conference to announce the plan, and ended his statement with an unequivocal declaration of confidence:

> The industry will be profitable. It will service its capital and it will pay dividends on the State's investment. It will in addition be an international industry because of its exports. We must grow into a highly market-oriented company with a capacity to find outlets for our products and literally and metaphorically to deliver the goods to satisfied customers domestically as well as overseas.[338]

Speaking to journalists later, Kevin underlined the fact that, going forward, the company 'will not operate with a cavalier attitude, that it can be bailed out by the Government, because within the EC, it can't. It must become viable in a very short time. We have to improve our processes, increase output, reduce costs, and extend our range and upgrade our quality.'[339]

While the development plan had received the go-ahead from the Government in February 1977, a series of unconnected events conspired to delay its implementation significantly.

Since 1971 pay adjustments had been governed by successive National Wage Agreements agreed between trade unions and employers in an effort to avoid a 'free for all' at a time of rising inflation. In 1976 the craft unions at ISH sought a 20 per cent differential above the top scale applicable to general workers. The Labour Court subsequently made recommendations, which were accepted by the company but rejected by the craft unions. In March 1977 an official strike was called, initially involving about ninety men, mostly electricians and fitters. Within a short time, however, the strike escalated, leading to virtually all of the staff being laid off. The strike lasted for six months and had the effect of almost paralysing the business, with the company losing sales worth more than £5 million. As a result, losses to June 1977 increased to over £2 million.

In June 1977 the coalition government, which had approved the £40 million development plan, was replaced by a Fianna Fáil Government. Given that Taoiseach Jack Lynch and his Cabinet colleague Gene Fitzgerald represented Cork constituencies, it was unlikely that the development plans for Haulbowline would meet with opposition. It was felt, however, that it would be prudent to have the plan re-evaluated in the context of the implications of the strike. Arthur D. Little, the company that had advised the Government on the original plan, confirmed that the initial projections were largely valid.

While the new Minister for Industry and Commerce, Desmond O'Malley, was being given time to consider the development plan, a potentially serious impediment arose. As required by law, the company had notified the European Commission of its plans at any early stage, so that the Commission could, if it so wished, express an opinion. On 21 December 1977 the Commission replied to Kevin in draft and in confidential terms. In its response, it expressed the view that capacity in the Community was likely to exceed demand in the medium term by a large margin. On that basis, the Commission invited ISH 'to reconsider the possibility of modernising the existing plant without any major increase in capacity'.[340] The Commission asserted that it was difficult, on economic grounds, to find arguments in favour of the proposed project and that the prospects for the export of section products from the new plant 'cannot be optimistic'.[341]

As the company was considering an appropriate response, the draft letter from the Commission was leaked to the media. The entire text of the letter was reproduced in *Business and Finance* magazine, which led with the assertion that the letter had 'the gravest importance not only to the 700 employees at Haulbowline but to the country as a whole. For what the Commission had said is, ought Ireland have a steel industry at all?'[342]

The rest of the media reportage was no less dramatic. 'The EEC has blocked an expansion bid by Irish Steel Holdings,' asserted the *Irish Press*, 'and it has told the firm, which employs 700 at its Haulbowline, Cobh, plant, that if the only alternative to expansion is closure, then it must go out of business.'[343] The article was accompanied by a photograph of Kevin above the caption, 'Man with a big problem'.

Magill magazine used the Commission letter as an opportunity to describe the proposed spending of £40 million against the backdrop of a world surplus in steel capacity as 'the essence of madness'. It continued: 'It is this kind of incompetent State investment that Ireland cannot afford, and by refusing to support the scheme, the EEC Commission has done Ireland a great favour.'[344]

In response, Kevin came out fighting. He informed *The Irish Times*[345] that the Commission could not stop the expansion and that the company could raise the necessary finance on the international markets if special, low-rate EEC loans were not forthcoming. 'The Chairman of ISH remained optimistic and instilled confidence,' recorded one commentator some years later. '… his resilience and combative spirit, proven so many times in his career, were more than ever necessary at this juncture in the fortunes of Irish Steel.'[346]

Behind the scenes, Kevin held a series of meetings with Commission officials. By December 1978 ISH had negotiated a deal with a French steel company, SMDN, whereby each company agreed to market a proportion of each other's production in their respective areas of market influence. While the arrangements did not have a significant impact on ISH's business, they served their purpose by allowing the Commission enough space to accept the company's development plan on the twin grounds that Ireland needed an efficient plant to meet domestic demands and that the new plant would produce a sufficiently wide range of products, compared to conventional mills, to ensure economic viability through exploration of export markets.

In late 1977, in anticipation of the importance that would attach to export markets, Kevin recruited Liam Coughlan as Chief Financial Officer on the understanding that he would later become Chief Executive. Coughlan had wide experience of exporting, having worked with Clover Meats. He became Chief Executive of ISH in 1980.

The placing of orders for equipment began in late 1978. Around the same time, following his retirement from his executive position at Irish Distillers, Kevin agreed to a request from Desmond O'Malley to become Executive Chairman of ISH for a two-year period to oversee the expansion. In fact, he remained in that role until January 1984, working closely with Liam Coughlan and his management team.

The company's losses continued to increase. By mid-1981, when the new facilities were completed, the company had accumulated losses of over £26 million. In addition, the cost of the development, originally estimated at £40 million, had spiralled to almost twice that amount, with £64 million as the actual cost of fixed assets and production expenses and a further £16 million required as working capital to cover the period from June 1978 to June 1986. Kevin gave as the reasons for the increase in cost the need to extend and modify the original design—which was, he said, the principal cause of the increase—delays in delivery, increased interest charges and interest rates and exchange losses due to the break with sterling. On top of all that, production at Haulbowline had effectively ceased for a full year to facilitate building works.[347]

In spite of Kevin's confidence and optimism, the immediate future for ISH looked no brighter. It was estimated that the level of overcapacity in steel production in Europe was 30 million tonnes. In addition, there was increasing competition for heavy steel from Japan, Korea and Brazil, while in the market for lighter steel, in which ISH operated, there was growing competition from Third World countries with cheap labour and energy costs.

The company sought funding from the Government of £50 million. Speaking at the AGM in November 1981, Kevin said that ISH was 'delicately balanced, very heavily burdened with debt, seeking substantial equity investment from the State at a time of severe economic constraints.'[348]

The economic difficulties faced by the country in 1981 had forced a number of State bodies to seek further Government support. The tightening economic situation was mirrored by extreme political instability. The Coalition Government, from whom funding was sought in October 1981, fell in February 1982. On the proposal of a new Minister for Industry and Energy, Albert Reynolds, a Government grant of £25 million to reduce the cumulative losses was approved in May 1982, bringing to £125 million the total amount made available by the Government to ISH since 1979 in the form of equity, grants and guaranteed borrowings.[349]

Throughout his time with Irish Steel, Kevin made a point of attending the annual World Steel Conference. In 1981 the Conference was held in Toronto. On the margins of the Conference the then Chairman of British Steel, Ian McGregor—who had been appointed to the role by Margaret Thatcher's government and was launching a major redundancy programme that would see employment in that company reduced by almost 100,000 in three years—declared that if he had his way, Irish Steel would be 'consigned to a bog'. When the comment was reported to Kevin, he was furious. He demanded to speak to McGregor and bluntly informed him that he should stick to dealing with British Steel's not insubstantial problems and not seek to interfere with the business of the company of which he, Kevin, was Chairman. Years later, McGregor, whose reputation as the hard man of British business was secured by his role as head of the British National Coal Board, confided that in all of his time at British Steel, the only man who ever stood up to him was Kevin McCourt.[350]

By November 1982 Kevin was again reporting that further State funding was required if the company was to survive. Losses for the year to June 1982 had been almost £22 million. On the same day as the company held its AGM, the third General Election in eighteen months was called. Writing in *The Irish Times* on 8 November 1982, the business journalist John Stanley expressed the view that while the company's directors 'may understandably feel that fate played an unfair trick by timing the facility to start coming on-stream just when the whole steel market is in turmoil ... however, [they] must remember that the public footing the bill for a mistimed investment are more than likely to hold them, rather than fate, responsible for the timing.'

In June 1983 the Minister for Industry and Energy, John Bruton, when bringing forward legislation to allow ISH borrow a further £25 million, warned that the level of borrowings was far too high and that corrective measures were required urgently. However, he also pointed out that the cost of closing ISH could be as high as £100 million. Later that month, in a letter to the Business Editor of *The Irish Times*, Kevin took issue with comments made in the newspaper:

> There is no doubt that the re-development of the Irish Steel plant has cost a lot of money. And it is true that it has not yet begun to pay off. But I think that, as a people, we should occasionally consider what we have achieved and take a respite from lamenting the inevitable cost.[351]

Two days later there was a collective sigh of relief in both ISH and the Government when the company was temporarily reprieved from massive cutbacks imposed on the rest of the European steel industry at what was reported to have been an acrimonious meeting of the European Commission. The Commission's decision to reduce capacity by 27 million tonnes was described as 'savage cutbacks, which amount to a political bombshell for many EEC governments'.[352]

The reprieve was only for six months. Meanwhile, Kevin continued to argue forcibly for further support for the business. Addressing a meeting of European steel stockists in Dublin, he declared: 'Steel is integral to any modern economy and because Irish Steel is the only plant of its kind in the country, it is not only a national asset, it is a national necessity.'[353]

The requirement of the Commission that all Community steel plants be self-sufficient by the end of 1985, and the reality that Irish Steel, if it was to have the opportunity of proving that its new plant could deliver that financial autonomy required further Government funding of £89 million, created an atmosphere of considerable anxiety in the first half of 1984. On a local level, the loss of 650 jobs in Cork, following quickly on the Ford and Dunlop closures, would have been disastrous.

On 22 June 1984 John Bruton confirmed that a package of £89 million would be made available, subject to Commission approval. The Government's case to Brussels was supported by a consultancy report, which forecast that the company should be able to return to profit in 1986. Kevin welcomed the commitment as 'Irish Steel's greatest opportunity and its last, last chance'.[354] Five days later, the Commission approved the Government's support for ISH on the basis that the recently modernised plant could return to profitability, in the right condition, which included revised production quotas. These were under consideration by the Council of Ministers who agreed in July to the revised quotas sought by the company.

While the accounts to June 1984 showed further losses of £23 million, the bulk of these, as with previous years, related to interest charges. Trading losses were well down and sales were up. Nonetheless, Kevin cautioned that even with the injection of £89 million, it would be 'foolish and reckless'[355] to assume that the company's difficulties had been overcome.

Although the Commission had decided to allow State aids to steel companies for a further year, up to the end of 1986, and although Kevin had suggested that a further £25 million was required, he recognised that the company needed to take steps to ensure its viability. In June 1985, on the back of further losses of £17 million, Kevin met with the company's trade unions. He informed them that the company needed 100 redundancies, a pay freeze for all employees and a strict cap on redundancy payments.

The unions rejected the proposals, accusing Kevin of using the old cliché of seeking to trim costs by sacrificing jobs[356] and of timing the announcement to coincide with the local elections. The leader of the Opposition, Charles Haughey, attacked Kevin's statement as 'extraordinary'. In relation to the suggestion that the announcement was connected to the local elections, he said:

> I would be reluctant to believe there would be anything as despicable as that involved although I have to say that the development is of such an unprecedented nature that it must give ground to some suspicions.[357]

The Government agreed with the approach adopted by the company and indicated that it would consider making a further £24 million available, but only on the basis that the company and its workforce reached agreement, within a month, on a pay freeze and redundancies.

Discussions with the trade unions began on 18 July. Kevin maintained the position that the company would close unless 115 workers were made redundant and the remainder accepted a pay freeze. The company increased the amount of the redundancy package on offer from one-and-a-half to two-and-a-half weeks' pay for every year of service, plus statutory entitlements. This offer was significantly less than the amounts paid to former Ford and Dunlop workers and was rejected by the unions.

The board of the company, led by Kevin, refused to move. The unions, assisted by the Labour Court, sought assistance from the EEC, which had a fund available for redundancy schemes in the steel industry. An editorial in *The Irish Times* summarised the position:

> In their handling of the crisis at Irish Steel the Government and the company's management have adroitly placed the unions in the position in which the survival of the plant appears to depend on the workers' willingness to come to terms with the economic realities of the industry.[358]

On 14 August the workforce rejected the company's proposal. Kevin warned that the situation was 'deadly serious' and accused the union leadership of 'gamesmanship'.[359] The Government maintained its position that the company would close after 21 August unless a deal was agreed.

As the deadline loomed, the Labour Court intervened and made recommendations that essentially supported the company's position, aligned with a proposal that the Government guarantee payments from the EEC Steelworkers Fund. On 22 August the workforce voted, by a majority of twenty-five, to reject the Court's recommendations. John Bruton announced the Government's decision to close the business. After further negotiations the Government agreed to postpone the decision until the following Monday, 26 August, provided a fresh ballot was held. The Government refused to agree to the full extent of the guarantee recommended by the Labour Court, placing the unions in the invidious position of being obliged to ballot members on a package inferior to that already rejected.

On the morning of the ballot, Taoiseach Garrett FitzGerald and Kevin appealed directly to the workforce. Faced with certain closure, the workforce voted, by a majority of 214, to accept the proposals and thereby save the business.

In parallel with seeking to achieve the cost reductions required, the company, at the request of the Government, spent a considerable amount of time during 1985 seeking joint venture partners. The Government recognised that external investment was essential given the prohibition on further State funding and that an alliance with a bigger company, one with stronger technical or marketing capability, could be valuable in ensuring the company's survival. Although no joint venture arrangement was consummated, John Bruton, speaking in the Dáil, paid 'a personal tribute to the Chairman, Mr. Kevin McCourt, for the work he has done in the company over the last few months and, in particular, for the personal effort he has put into this joint venture activity which had to be undertaken, alongside other internal matters.'[360] Later, in the Seanad, he reiterated that Kevin had 'devoted prodigious efforts to travelling all over the world to meet potential joint venture partners.'[361] In reality, by this stage quite a lot of the travelling on behalf of the company was undertaken by Liam Coughlan and a board member, John Byrne.

On 2 January 1986, Kevin announced that after eleven eventful years, he was stepping down as Chairman of Irish Steel. Over the following decade there were many more crises and false dawns. In 1996 the State transferred the entire ownership of the company to ISPAT International, a multinational business founded in India, for a nominal sum. Five years later, the business closed.

Chapter 8

The Non-Executive Director

Throughout his career Kevin was in constant demand as a non-executive director. The thirty-seven year span from his first appointment to the board of the IDA in 1949 to his retirement from Irish Steel in 1986 saw him serve on eighteen different boards: four in the public service, three in banking and insurance and eleven in industrial businesses. Since many of these overlapped, he was able to say, with some pride, that he had in total 109 board member years, of which thirty-nine were as Chairman. 'People ask you,' he once explained, 'and it is not easy to decline!'[362]

The role of director was one that Kevin cherished. In an address to the Institute of Directors in Ireland in November 1986, he reflected on his career as a company director:

> I love being a director. I admire and respect the position. I regret that it carries connotations of privilege, security and wealth. On the contrary, it is a position of trust and constructive involvement for the better advancement of the affairs of a company. Sometimes it is a role that attracts contumely and disrespect. This last is a weakness of the statutory machinery for the creation of companies in that, by a very simple legal expedient, unworthy persons can become directors and by mendacity and

irresponsibility bring the generality of the role into disrepute.[363]

Kevin then offered his audience his views on the qualities required to be a non-executive director:

> ... style, appearance, personality, a reasonable expectation of fitting in. I do not mean by that old tie or peer group origin. Board relations are more permanent than marriage. It is nearly impossible without harm to the company to persuade a person who has emerged as difficult or incompatible to leave the board just because he is not fitting in. So prejudge carefully yours and his reasonable expectations of getting on together.
>
> He should be a businessman in the broad sense, irrespective of his specialisation and training. If he or she has a record of success in life, it is more than likely that the common sense of business judgement has been acquired.
>
> I think that age is irrelevant. What is too old or too young – these are only accidental numbers on a birth register. What is important is health, capacity to give time, ability to contribute, visible performance in job, career or profession.
>
> Courage and common sense are great qualities. Common sense is the basis of good judgement. Courage comes from experience, from controlled self-confidence, the willingness to be heard, seen and counted. Courage, too, is about being human, having strong feelings, being able to reach human beings and their problems, being understanding, supportive in criticism and sensitive to human frailty, but persistent in the seeking of excellence in performance.[364]

He emphasised the critical relationship between the board and management, and the importance of a proper balance between the two:

> The director on the board is a partner with management in bringing about that degree of change which is desirable for the business. I think the director must be supportive of management. It must not be blind or casual support, but rather be based on belief and confidence in management, based on factual assessment that management is doing what reasonably and practically reflects the courses of action the management proposed when they presented the operating profit plan or the new venture for the board's endorsement.
>
> It is not the board's job to upstage management or to propose optional courses of action which, if forced or persuaded on management, shift the singularity of responsibility of management to manage and perform satisfactorily.
>
> Effectively to contribute to his abilities and knowledge, a board member should understand the business, that is, what it does and by what means and for what purpose. He must also be well read on the company, he should be analytical, he should require clarification where there is uncertainty. He should act for the purpose of satisfying himself that management is performing as expected, that the results are as forecast. He must be insistent on explanations for departures from the norm or the projected.
>
> This is not to outdo management nor to disprove them. It is to satisfy himself that management – they being human too – did not overstate the prospects or underestimate the resources needed. He must satisfy himself that management

is not over-confident, that it continues to be sound in its judgement, that it does not fail to react decisively to those changing circumstances I mentioned earlier.

Managements of business become possessive. Successful management may suffer from the seduction of success. This leads to latent resistance and the fear of interference. It leads to egotism in management, to a reluctance to disclose. The sense of possessiveness as an expression of pride and performance is commendable. It is less commendable when it is an expression of self flattery. Flattery is all very fine unless you inhale it.

So, an important contribution of the board is finding out one's satisfied knowledge. Holding information tight to the chest by management is a paradox of behaviour be it arrogance or self-protection. The board should counter by showing management that the board is supportive, but does mean to know about its company and will not be left uncertain and in the dark.[365]

Kevin's contract with P.J. Carroll's specifically provided for his serving on other boards. During his time in Dundalk, he joined the boards of a number of local companies. One of these was Dundalk Engineering Works Ltd, a company established in 1957, on the initiative of Seán Lemass as Minister for Industry and Commerce, to lease railway engineering workshops from the Great Northern Railway. This was done in an attempt to protect the employment of over 1,000 men, whose jobs were threatened by a reduction in rail services on both sides of the border. In commenting on the initiative the local newspaper, the *Dundalk Democrat*, expressed the hope that 'the wide experience of world market possibilities which Mr. McCourt has gained will be of immense value to the new undertaking.'[366] The company received an unexpected boost in 1958 when it was chosen as the worldwide manufacturer of the three-wheeled motor car, Heinkel.

Kevin's role as Director-General of RTÉ prevented him from having any involvement in outside businesses. When he joined United Distillers, he accepted a number of appointments. Three of these were public service roles at the request of different Government ministers.

In 1965 he was appointed as a member of the Council of Gorta, which was established in that year under the aegis of the Department of Agriculture. Its origins were in the Irish Freedom from Hunger Campaign, set up in 1960 by the Irish Red Cross Society in response to an international call by the United Nations. At the request of the Minister for Agriculture, Neil Blaney, Kevin became Chairman in 1969. By this time Gorta was involved in twenty-two projects, mainly in Africa.

Kevin's contacts in RTÉ and with the media in general were put to good effect on the charity's behalf. A film entitled *Gorta at Work* was commissioned to highlight the organisation's work in Tanzania and Kenya, with Eamonn Andrews agreeing to act as narrator. The *Radharc* team at RTÉ, under Fr Joe Dunn, made a further film, *Gorta Gives a Dam*. In his role as Chairman, Kevin was co-opted by the hierarchy onto the newly established Commission for Justice and Peace. He also represented Gorta at the United Nations-sponsored World Food Congress.

Although in 1972 Kevin agreed a second three-year term as Chairman of Gorta, his other commitments forced him to stand down the following year. Noting his resignation, the Minister for Agriculture, Mark Clinton, said that Kevin's 'national image, business acumen, wide experience and contacts had become a great asset to Gorta and one which he allowed the organisation to exploit generously.'[367]

A second State-sponsored board to which Kevin was appointed was Fóir Teoranta. It began operations in April 1972 and its function was to provide reconstruction finance for potentially viable businesses unable to raise capital from normal commercial sources. It was, as Kevin once described it, 'the last resort of industries on the brink of disaster'.[368] He was appointed to the position by George Colley, Minister for Finance in the Fianna Fáil Government of the time. Two years later, a Labour Party Minister in a Coalition Government appointed him as Chairman of Irish Steel.

In addition to the board of Fóir Teoranta, the year 1972 saw Kevin take on his first significant commercial non-executive appointment. In anticipation of Ireland joining the EEC in the following year, the major Dutch bank Algemene Bank Nederland (ABN) became the first continental European bank to open a branch in Ireland. The board of the Irish bank was chaired by T.J. O'Driscoll, formerly of Bord Fáilte. Kevin was joined on the board by Edmund Williams, a prominent businessman from Tullamore, and subsequently by the industrialist Jefferson Smurfit Snr, then Chairman of Jefferson Smurfit Group. Later additions to the board were Howard Kilroy, Chief Operations Officer at Smurfit Group, and the former Taoiseach, Jack Lynch. Kevin proved to be an important addition to the Algemene board, with his knowledge and understanding of the Dutch approach to business, from his time at Hunter Douglas, proving to be of considerable help to his board colleagues.

By the end of the 1970s ABN's decision to establish in Ireland appeared to have been an excellent one. Its pre-tax profits for the year 1979 were over £1.6 million, up 30 per cent on the previous year. In June 1980 Kevin succeeded O'Driscoll as Chairman, a position he held until his retirement from the board in 1985.

The boost in profits proved short-lived, however, and Kevin's accession to the chair coincided with the beginning of a sharp downturn in the Irish economy. The Bank's principal lending was to semi-State businesses and to the manufacturing industry; it had a policy of not lending to the property sector. While the semi-State business remained robust, demand for money from manufacturing was in decline. By 1981 profits had reduced, principally as a result of the introduction of a Government bank levy. In his report to the AGM, Kevin declared:

> We protested to the Minister for Finance regarding this arbitrary and inequitable tax which bore no relation to profitability. The levy was particularly distressing in our case since it represented an additional charge of over 12½% on profits which had already fallen for taxation in the usual manner. The proposal in the recent budget to quadruple the levy is a matter of the gravest concern.[369]

Over the next few years, ABN hovered between modest losses and equally modest profits. In 1984 the Bank reported a fairly significant loss, caused primarily by bad debts in the agriculture and agri-related sectors, although the business improved significantly in subsequent years.

In late 1977, following the announcement of his impending retirement from his executive role at IDG, Kevin was invited to join the board of Jefferson Smurfit Group plc. Given his unswerving belief in the need for Irish businesses to think globally rather than locally, it was fitting that he should join the board of what was widely recognised as Ireland's first multinational company.

Founded in 1938 by his colleague from the ABN board, Jefferson Smurfit Snr, the company, which had floated on the Irish Stock Exchange in 1964 and on the London Exchange five years later, was already a significant international player in the manufacture of paper board and packaging products by the time Kevin joined the board. Michael Smurfit, who had become Chairman and Chief Executive of the company following the unexpected death of his father in March 1977, had ambitious plans for further expansion. In 1974 the company had made its first entry into the United States through the acquisition of a 40 per cent stake in Time Industries Inc., in Chicago. In 1977 it completed a full takeover of Time Industries and the following year acquired a majority stake in Alton Box Board Company.

The business continued to grow rapidly throughout the 1980s. Michael Smurfit recalls that during this period, Kevin's contribution to the board was immense:

> He was the de facto senior independent director at a time when that role did not formally exist. He was a class act, always meticulously prepared for board meetings, always knowing the right question to ask. He was an extraordinary man who had a way with him that was very special. He was an exceptional board member who brought real value to the company.[370]

For his part, Kevin relished the international dimension of the Smurfit business, travelling on behalf of the company to Latin America and Australia, among other places. He also liked the fact that he could walk from his home in Donnybrook to board meetings at the nearby Smurfit headquarters.

In January 1981 Kevin became a founder director of a new life insurance company, Life Association Ireland (LAI). Although a new company, the business had been established in Ireland in 1844 as an agency network. In 1985 LAI merged with the life element of Hibernian Insurance to form Hibernian Life Association. Kevin became Chairman of Hibernian Life in

November 1986 following the retirement of Lord Killanin, and remained as Chairman of the company until his retirement in April 1989, when he was replaced by his colleague from the ABN Board, Edmund Williams.

By 1990, as he celebrated his seventy-fifth year, Kevin had relinquished virtually all of his directorships. Although he missed his involvement on boards, he felt that the time had come for him to draw the curtain on his business career. It was not that he felt too old—he had always believed that age was irrelevant in business. However, this philosophy had equally encouraged him to make way for younger talent. When people remarked that Richard Burrows, at thirty-two, was very young to take over at Irish Distillers, Kevin would reply that that was something time alone would cure!

There was to be one further board appointment, however. In 1998, as he approached his eighty-third birthday, Kevin was asked by Dermot Desmond to join the board of Baltimore Technologies. Desmond had first got to know Kevin in the 1970s when Kevin was Managing Director of IDG and Desmond was an executive with Investment Bank of Ireland. In the intervening years the two came to know each other well, with Dermot Desmond coming to view Kevin as a friend as well as a mentor.

In 1996, when Desmond was already one of Ireland's most successful entrepreneurs, he invested in a small, six-person IT consultancy firm called Baltimore Technologies. The firm had been identified by Desmond's colleague, Fran Rooney, who was seeking a vehicle for what he saw as the biggest business opportunity of the time: security for electronic commerce. The company was successful in winning a significant contract put out to tender by the European Commission, which proved to be a crucial kickstart. Other important contracts followed, most notably with banks and with the NHS in Britain.

As the ambitions of the company grew—Rooney's mantra was 'GBF' (Get Big Fast)—Dermot Desmond recognised the need for an experienced, independent director with no vested interest, who would, in his words, 'question everything'. Kevin was delighted to be approached to join the board of such a dynamic, fast-growing company. He relished being back at the boardroom table years after he had chosen to leave the corporate stage. 'He brought great order, great discipline to the board,' recalls Dermot Desmond. 'He questioned the product, the vision, the marketing strategy, but always in a supportive way.'[371]

A number of months after Kevin joined the board, Baltimore Technologies completed a reverse takeover of a much larger British public company, Zergo, which was listed on the London Stock Exchange. On the following day the company had a major publicity coup when President Bill Clinton and Taoiseach Bertie Ahern attached electronically generated signatures to a joint communiqué on e-commerce, using technology developed by Baltimore. With the company planning a listing on Nasdaq, Kevin felt he had made his contribution and retired from the board. Baltimore went on to soar to amazing heights before crashing, equally spectacularly.

Chapter 9

A Reflection

On the occasion of his retirement from his position as Managing Director of IDG, Kevin gave a lengthy interview to Professor Ivor Kenny, which was published in the magazine of the Irish Management Institute, on whose board Kevin had served. In that interview he gave an insight into the values and principles that had underpinned and driven his career.

On what constitutes success in a business career and on the sacrifices that must be made in its pursuit, he said:

> I am never sure how you measure success. So far as I am concerned, it is not monetary success. I suppose it is the success of being wanted as a chief executive and the feeling that I have made some contribution to the activities that I have been involved in. The price is being alone a good deal, of long, long work and travelling hours – at the expense of hours that could be spent with your family.
>
> If your job requires total involvement, then you have to make up your mind that you have got to sacrifice what other people have as a social life. I am a member of a golf club and, even at this stage of my life, this is the fifth successive year I have not set foot in it.
>
> I don't know any chief executive who is not holding the reins of a team of galloping horses. I don't know anybody

who is doing that who is not putting his whole life and soul into it. To do that, you must have a domestic situation which understands it, accepts it, and I have been blessed with that.[372]

On the importance of experience:

I certainly would not play down experience. There is nothing wrong with age, be it elderly or very young, as long as the talent and capacity are there. Experience is all important. There is no substitute for it. It does not come with youth. It only comes with living, with finding out, with doing and being done by - and being done at.[373]

And on whether the measure of a man is the size of his problems:

You can't run your job without having problems. Nobody sits where you are or where I am sitting in Bow Street without having problems. That's what you are there for. You are the man standing in the middle of a confluence of rivers. Every one of them within itself is a problem and every one of them has a man in that river who is looking to you to solve his problem his way. He is not interested in the problems of the other people, but all those rivers, all those people, all those problems are the totality of your responsibility.[374]

Kevin McCourt is universally remembered by those who knew him with admiration, respect and affection: admiration for his skills as a businessman, respect for the values that underpinned his career and his life and affection for a man who, in the words of his daughter, Pamela, was 'charismatic, charming, cultured, happy, unfailingly smiling, courteous and kind'.[375]

He can fairly be described as one of the first truly professional managers in Irish business and as one of its most distinguished leaders. No one else in Irish business could point to a career at the top, spanning over four decades and incorporating such diverse industries as tobacco, broadcasting, distilling and steel. Regardless of the industry involved, regardless of whether the business was State-owned or family-dominated, whether centuries old or just starting out, Kevin approached each role with the same all-consuming drive, pragmatism and desire to be successful. He was international and global in his outlook before most others in Irish business became so, and he was a pioneer in advocating the critical importance of marketing, advertising and brand awareness and the imperative of seeking out export markets.

Above all else, Kevin brought to each position he held an enormous personal and professional integrity. He had an innate sense of what was right, what was proper and what was fair. He liked to quote Mark Twain: '… you should always do what is right – it will please a few, and astonish the rest.' He was very straightforward in his dealings—'you always knew where you stood with him', is a common refrain from former business colleagues. He had little interest in money; personal gain was never on his agenda.

He was a deeply patriotic man who loved and was proud of Ireland. This is best summed up in a quote from him when he said: 'I have worked for many years in Ireland for my family and myself with always a growing sense of owing something to my country. I have worked in Ireland for me and my family in the 1930s, 40s, half of the 50s, the 60s and 70s and am happy to be still doing so with the debt not yet paid to my country for what it has made available to me.'[376]

As a manager, Kevin led by example. He had a huge work

ethic, was invariably first to arrive at work and among the last to leave. He worked long hours throughout his career; each Saturday, if not spent at the office, was largely given over to meetings with colleagues at his home to chew over recent developments and plan strategies. 'I suppose I work, on average, about eighty hours a week,' he once told an interviewer.[377]

He was intolerant of people who took things for granted or expected others to provide for them: 'One of the problems we've got is that people don't put in enough shoe-leather and hard work. Doing your best is not good enough. We have to do what is necessary.'[378]

He was a demanding leader, not slow to express dissatisfaction if a piece of work failed to meet his expectations. He had little time for people who did not strive for excellence and abhorred sloppiness, mental or physical. He could be ruthless when the situation demanded it, but never at the expense of knowingly hurting or ridiculing others. He avoided apportioning blame in public and lived by the creed that the buck stopped with him. He could, and did, recognise when he was wrong and was never too proud to admit a mistake and apologise.

He had a great understanding of the human condition and a capacity to assess people and situations very quickly. He was extremely decisive. A number of his former colleagues who reported directly to him recall that if a proposal required a decision from Kevin, it was usually forthcoming within twenty-four hours. He was fond of saying that decisions were easy when you had the right information, and that you might as well make a decision as there would be an outcome whether you did or not.

Kevin provoked great loyalty in those who worked for him. While hierarchical in his attitude to management structures, he remained approachable and down-to-earth in his dealings with colleagues. He made a point of getting around the production facilities—whether visiting all the distilleries before he joined IDG or making his way up mountains, in snow, to meet the men in charge of RTÉ masts—so that he could understand, at firsthand, the challenges his employees and, by extension, the business faced. He attended as many staff social functions around the country as he could, invariably being among the last to leave as he entertained his colleagues with a song, frequently one from the repertoire of Count John McCormack, his favourite singer, delivered in his own impressive tenor voice.

He worked hard, though not always successfully, at remembering the names of as many employees as possible and could surprise people by his ability to recall, and show genuine interest in, aspects of their lives outside work, whether the names of their children or their obscure hobbies. This was assisted by a practice of keeping pieces of information stored on a rolodex card system for use the next time he was due to meet someone.

As well as the self-evident management skills Kevin brought to each role, he also brought a sense of style. He took great pride in his appearance: his elegant Italian suits, his collection of bow ties, the rose in his buttonhole and, even more obviously, his trademark red socks, which set him apart from his peers from a very early stage. He had his hair trimmed virtually every Saturday by the barber in the Shelbourne Hotel. His car, usually a Mercedes, was always spotlessly clean.

His pipe served as an important prop, with some recalling how his personal assistant would be seen on occasion marching in front of him, carrying an enormous ash-tray that would be placed ceremonially on the rostrum in advance of Kevin entering a room to speak. When he addressed the Advertising Press Club in 1968 without a pipe in evidence, one commentator reported the following day that 'Kevin McCourt without his pipe, like Samson without his hair, is not the same man at all at all.'[379] His profile as a prominent pipe-smoker no doubt contributed to his appointment to the board of directors of Peterson Tennant, a public company that included the pipe manufacturer, Kapp & Peterson.

He was an impressive public speaker, who loved discovering new and unusual words, which he recorded in a book, along with jokes and anecdotes, for use in one of his carefully crafted speeches.

Education was a recurring theme throughout his life. To attend good schools and universities was his ambition for his family and was also his advice to many people throughout his life. He ensured that the companies he led enabled people to have access to the best management training courses available. His belief in further education undoubtedly stemmed from his own experience as a young man when a similar opportunity was not available to him. If it had been, he often said, he would have been a lawyer, probably a barrister.

He was extremely cultured, a voracious reader, when time allowed, and a lover of theatre, classical music and opera. He was a patron of the Dublin Theatre Festival and had a particular fondness for the poetry of Francis Ledwidge. Surprisingly, for a former Director-General of RTÉ, he rarely watched television, other than to view international rugby matches.

He was intellectually very curious and was fascinated by languages. He was a good Irish speaker and took Dutch, French and finally Italian courses, imposing on himself, in later life, meticulous and gruelling hours of study and repetition. His grandson, Orson, recalls how he would spend up to fifteen hours a day going over Italian verbs, writing them out hundreds and hundreds of times. That said, his study of Italian could not reasonably be described as hardship, given that it involved lengthy stays in Florence, where he delighted not only in his studies but also in the *dolce vita*. He had a particular love of Italian wine and cheeses. On one occasion he wrote to his granddaughter, Melissa:

> I am looking forward to going back to Italy. It is a sort of escape – is that a defence? I love being at school, and being free, and meeting new – and young – people. They all accept me as one of themselves.[380]

In his youth Kevin had been a proficient rugby player, winning Minor and Metropolitan Cup medals with Blackrock R.F.C. He also enjoyed playing cricket in Pembroke Cricket Club—what his father thought of his interest in these 'foul foreign games' is not recorded!—and was also, for a time, a flyweight boxer. He was a good golfer, but had to give it up because it took up so much time. He was a regular, and strong, swimmer in the Fitzwilliam LTC pool.

His true passion, however, was fly fishing, a hobby he took up when at Carroll's, spending many happy hours on the River Boyne. Later, many of his holidays were designed around fishing, often in the company of Tom O'Higgins and his family in the West of Ireland, staying at the Angler's Rest in Headford or, later still, expeditions with his great friend, Jack Lynch. His children and grandchildren recall that his determination was such that he would stay fishing for hours in the hope that 'one more go' would yield results.

He was an avid gardener, spending happy hours tending his beloved roses or planting vegetables, particularly tomatoes. In 1979 he and Peggy bought Harmony Cottage, a unique Spanish-style villa on Eglington Road, in Dublin, and it was there, in his later years, that his passion for gardening really took off.

Kevin had many friends across many countries, interests and

backgrounds. His engaging personality drew people to him. He retained and maintained those friendships over the years through the generous hospitality offered by him and Peggy, coupled with his great talent for writing letters.

During the last seven years of his life Kevin would meet regularly with two of his lifelong friends, Tom Roche and Gearoid Crookes. All three of them had attended Blackrock College. He and Tom Roche also lived near each other in Sandymount. Kevin often told the story of how, after they had left school, Roche told him he was going to buy a truck to go into business and asked if Kevin would like to join with him as a partner. Financial constraints prevented that happening and he used to laugh at what might have been: Tom Roche went on to establish Roadstone and become one of Ireland's most successful entrepreneurs.

The three friends would meet every Sunday evening at 6.00pm in Tom Roche's house, Chesterfield, for a couple of hours and that commitment was sacrosanct. The importance of that friendship is best appreciated by the inscription on the three silver salvers Kevin commissioned in recognition of the tradition that was so important to each of them:

> Tom, Gearoid and Kevin, three dear friends from school days – on this day we thank the Lord that the aggregate of our ages is 250 years and that we can enjoy weekly in Tom's home a getting together with humour, laughter, happiness, tales abounding and we hope a measure of wisdom.
>
> The times we lived in and the circumstances of our professional and business careers enabled us to make some contribution to Ireland. For that too dear Lord we are thankful.

Although he had many and varied interests and was blessed

with a large circle of friends, Kevin McCourt had two consuming passions in life: his career and, way above all else, his family. He was a demonstratively affectionate father to his four children and a wonderful mentor, adviser and friend to each of them. He had a terrific sense of fun and 'of the ridiculous', as Peggy used to put it. He took a keen interest in each of his ten grandchildren. His first grandchild, Conal, recalls him as someone who always offered thoughtful, measured advice, who never gave instructions on what to do but steered his listeners in the right direction so that they could make their own decisions. No birthday or other special occasion passed without the receipt of one of Kevin's distinctive letters. He would regularly have lunch with his grandchildren, catching up on what was happening in their lives while imparting some wisdom to them.

And, of course, there was Peggy. She was the love of Kevin's life and he of hers. All that he achieved in his career would not have been possible without her unqualified support and understanding. While she did not enjoy the media attention occasionally afforded to her by virtue of her husband's high profile, she proved herself adept at dealing with interviewers in a warm and courteous manner. 'Mrs. McCourt presents an unruffled and serene attitude,' reported one interviewer, 'and never appears to be in what my American colleagues call "a tizzy".'[381]

Peggy also showed considerable business flair. When living in Dundalk in the early 1950s, she started a company, Deirdre Designs, making Irish souvenirs—West of Ireland scenes painted on machined turf and traditional Irish dolls, to mention two of her products. In one year they were chosen for Harrods' Christmas tree and she was proud to have Macy's in New York as one of her regular customers. She was a talented artist, painting each item she sold herself.

Kevin and Peggy were a very close couple, their preference always to be together at home rather than anywhere else. Tragically, Peggy was very unwell for a number of years before Kevin died, a fact with which he never really came to terms. Those were lonely and difficult times for him.

In early April 2000, just short of his eighty-fifth birthday, Kevin suffered a stroke from which he never recovered. He passed away on 13 May. His funeral service was held in Donnybrook Church. Speaking to a large gathering of his father's business colleagues and friends, Declan McCourt recalled Kevin as a remarkable and affectionate man who had introduced his children to travel, art and music. 'He was never constrained by the boundaries of his environment and he encouraged us to do the same.'

A tribute was also paid by Howard Kilroy, who had first come to know Kevin as a fellow board member at Algemene Bank and later when Kevin served on the Smurfit board. Kevin was, in Howard Kilroy's words, 'a father figure and a role model who was, in the truest sense, an honourable man'.

Among the many letters the McCourt family received following Kevin's death were tributes from some of Ireland's leading businessmen. Jim Culleton described Kevin as 'the first of a new breed of professional entrepreneurs in Ireland'. Tony O'Reilly echoed this sentiment, saying that Kevin was 'the first of his breed – the new Elizabethans that chartered the way towards the prosperity we all enjoy today', while Michael Smurfit recalled that Kevin's advice 'was always exceptional'. A friend recalled that Kevin had 'the saving grace of a splendid, often mischievous, sense of humour to smooth the often tortuous way'.

In a piece published in *The Irish Times* on 5 June 2000, his friend for over fifty years, T.F. O'Higgins, recorded that:

... despite his multitude of activities, he always had a listening ear and valuable advice for those facing some personal problem, big or small, and his friendships lasted despite gaps in years and despite the different directions which lives might take ... Meeting Kevin was always enjoyable. He was a good conversationalist and an accomplished raconteur ... Kevin's ability to bring people together would come into play and his wit, humour and anecdotes would soon melt shyness and reserve and bring smiles to the sternest of faces. His table, presided over by the loveable Peggy, always carried such delicacies of food and wine as to ruin even the strictest of diets.

The story of how Ireland matured, in the second half of the twentieth century, from an insular, economically despondent country to a self-confident, successful nation has been told on many occasions in recent years. The role played by individual politicians and public servants in that transformation has been generously and rightly lauded. The contribution of individual business leaders to this cause has not been as fully recognised, however. Many of them were pioneers in their time and deserve to have their names on the roll of Ireland's honour. One of these—a man who, throughout his long career, set the example for a new, self-believing, upfront, stylish and internationally focussed Ireland—was a Kerryman: Kevin C. McCourt.

Appendix

Address by Kevin McCourt to the Institute of Directors in Ireland, 12 November 1986

Mr Chairman and Gentlemen,

I thank you for the compliment of your invitation to speak to you today. I find that over 38 years I have been a board member of 18 companies. Four of these were in the public service (IDA, CTT, Foir Teoranta, Gorta), three were in banking and insurance, eleven were industrial. Since many of them overlapped, they totalled to 109 board member years of which 39 were Chairman years. I do not offer these facts as any kind of record or special achievement.

My subject is the role of the director in a changing world. Since the world of business is always changing, so changes the role of the director. I use the word 'role' to embrace among other contributions, involvement, study, time-giving, learning about the business, recognition of legal and moral responsibilities.

There is the director solus, a person. There is the director collectively – a part of the board. There is that director who also carried the additional burden and responsibility of being a chairman. Each category imposes obligations with an inter-play of relations between all three.

I love being a director. I admire and respect the position. I regret that it carries connotations of privilege, security and wealth. On the contrary, it is a position of trust and constructive involvement for the better advancement of the affairs of a company. Sometimes it is a role that attracts contumely and disrespect. This last is a weakness of the statutory machinery for the creation of companies in that, by a very simple legal expedient, unworthy persons can become directors and by mendacity and irresponsibility bring the generality of the role into disrepute.

Directors are a statutory invention arising out of the creation of the joint stock company, the company of limited liability. Directors are those legally responsible for the effective management and achievement of the corporate entity's objectives.

Neglect is committed by individuals, not by fictitious creations like boards of companies. Total responsibility must be laid with individuals. Putting it another way, the source of the obligations of a company is the acts of its agents acting in that capacity. These are the directors and they personally are responsible.

Interestingly, the Act contains no detailed definition of the term director. In fact, it describes a director as any person occupying the position of director by whatever name called. In the English Act, there are certain purposes for which the term includes a person in accordance with whose directives or instructions the directors are accustomed to act. The Chartered Institute of Secretaries suggests that professional advisors will not usually be treated as being directors if they restrict their functions to advising the company, leaving the board of directors to make the final decision.

However, if they become more closely involved in attendance

at board meetings, even though not entitled to vote, and if it seems that they might influence the decisions reached by the directors, they might be regarded as occupying the position of a director.

I imagine that the connotation of privilege stems from the fact that for many generations directors came from a single class. They were the stakeholders in companies. They were from the same social background as the promoters or founders.

For long years, directors represented stakeholders only – themselves and those who brought them into their companies. Even with the growth of the public company and the vast range of new investor categories, directors still joined boards because they were socially understood and acceptable to those already there.

One imagines that the bases of selection were:

Is he one of us?

How old is he?

Where did he go to school?

Not:

What is his performance?

How young is he?

Is he a businessman?

What will he bring to our deliberations?

That first stilted blind way of choosing a board member has declined by time, but it is not extinguished by any means. We all lean towards those who seem to be like us.

Reflective of the privilege board was the subservient position of the secretary:-

> While the great ones repair to their dinner, the secretary sits getting thinner and thinner, racking his brains to record and report, what he thinks that they think they ought to have thought.

The investor stakeholder is no longer the sole consideration of the directors' contribution. We know that the employees are stakeholders, and creditors, institutional investors, customers, suppliers, the community with which our company is associated, our legal advisors and our auditors.

Not all of them can be specifically represented on the board for their greater protection. But they have rights. Most of them are legal rights and he who is a director has an accountability to be aware of those rights. In Germany, for social or political reasons, there is a board worker representation. In Sweden, there is representation of government. In the United States, there is a lobby for board representation to include minority interests and disadvantageously placed groups such as women, the poor, non-whites, and others.

As you know, it is declared policy of organised labour in Ireland to require worker board representation in our companies. It obtains already in many of the State enterprises. I did not have worker directors on the board of Irish Steel in the eleven years I was Chairman there. I would not have objected to it. I think it would add to effective communication, but I am sure that it also makes problems in the boardroom about confidentiality and strategic timing of information giving.

There is no use in my saying that all directors act to the desirable standards. Not because they have criminal tendencies, but because they may be the wrong men or women with the wrong company, appointed for the wrong reason, maybe they are just plain lazy or they are too busy elsewhere.

So what should we be doing about it? I think all I could say is that we should think and talk about board directorships with the same degree of analysis, job description and selectivity we give to hiring a production manager or a financial controller.

Choosing only from those whom we know is perpetuating

peer grouping, the comfort of conformity. Some years ago, I saw an advertisement in the *Economist* for a non-executive director. I thought this was a breakthrough in that fortress of tradition. I do not recall seeing another such. Incidentally, I answered that particular advertisement, and was sobered in my presumption by the most effective of all reactions – no reply.

It is impossible to state any ground rules about the manner of choosing and the choice of directors. The multiplicity of variations in need and circumstances, in shape, size and character of companies, the personal assessment, the perceived need, and the choice are all subjective.

Let me offer thoughts from experience. I think smaller rather than larger boards are more effective. Either as a board member or as a chairman of the board when it comes to talk about a non-executive director, I have always looked for what I call personal amenity.

By this I mean style, appearance, personality, a reasonable expectation of fitting in. I do not mean by that old tie or peer group origin. Board relations are more permanent than marriage. It is nearly impossible without harm to the company to persuade a person who has emerged as difficult or incompatible to leave the board just because he is not fitting in. So prejudge carefully yours and his reasonable expectations of getting on together.

Given that board membership is greater in responsibility than in privilege, the potential newcomer must have the time for it bearing in mind that pre-board preparation time may be twice or more than that of board meeting duration – that is, if the board meetings are efficiently conducted.

He should be a businessman in the broad sense, irrespective of his specialisation and training. If he or she has a record of success in life, it is more than likely that the common sense of business judgement has been acquired.

I do not think that the best directors are your favourite banker, financial advisor or lawyer. If they are good in those capacities, why blunt their objectivity with the domesticities and the conflicts of business. That is not to say that bankers, accountants and lawyers do not make good directors. What I am saying is that you should choose directors for being good professionals with overriding business sense or just good proven businessmen and not because they are specialist advisors. It also makes it harder to change them as professional advisors if they are also board members.

I think that age is irrelevant. What is too old or too young – these are only accidental numbers on a birth register. What is important is health, capacity to give time, ability to contribute, visible performance in job, career or profession.

Courage and common sense are great qualities. Common sense is the basis of good judgement. Courage comes from experience, from controlled self-confidence, the willingness to be heard, seen and counted. Courage, too, is about being human, having strong feelings, being able to reach human beings and their problems, being understanding, supportive in criticism and sensitive to human frailty, but persistent in the seeking of excellence in performance.

Without getting into definitions of the word, I think experience is of lesser importance than evidence of performance. The purist would argue that, in the strict sense, if experience is the knowledge of how to act or advise in a set of circumstances, it is valid only if exactly the same set of circumstances arises again. Shaw said that experience is the name we give our mistakes. I think experience also comes from our achievements.

Whatever we do, we are concerned with people, resources and variable circumstances. The first two, people and resources, are reasonably constant; at least their variability is measurable and predictable. But changing circumstances are different in degree every day. That is their very nature, they do change and the same pattern of a situation is never the same between one day and another. We all know that the problem intractable of resolution on one day is often resolved on another day, not always because we have the light of the Holy Ghost in the meantime, but because a change in the circumstances and elements of the problem simplified finding its resolution.

So if you spend some part of your life wrestling with changing circumstances, worse ones as well as better, you learn adroitness, understanding, a facility to measure what you can or should do, you learn how to handle the resisting force wrestling with you.

We all do this all the time in all businesses with varying degrees of success. Our success translates into visible performance in what we are charged with doing. That is a far wider and deeper reservoir of capacity and adaptability than experience presumed to have been acquired simply by lapse of time and by having been around in different places.

Change is the one constant in business. Four hundred years ago, Machiavelli wrote that it should be borne in mind that there is nothing more difficult to arrange, more doubtful of success, and more dangerous to carry out than initiating change.

Three hundred years later, Emerson wrote about Collins the lighthouse builder and of how he found obstinate resistance to a project to build a lighthouse on a United States coastline 'as it would injure the wrecking business'. Still later the Duke of Wellington in Parliament opposed the expansion of the Railway system in England because he said it would encourage the working classes to move about.

These illustrations are probably extreme in relation to my theme that change is the one and most opposed constant in business. It is the function of management to foresee enforced change as well as to initiate change for the better promotion of business objectives.

The director on the board is a partner with management in bringing about that degree of change which is desirable for the business. I think the director must be supportive of management. It must not be blind or casual support, but rather be based on belief and confidence in management, based on factual assessment that management is doing what reasonably and practically reflects the course of action the management proposed when they presented the operating profit plan or the new venture for the board's endorsement.

It is not the board's job to upstage management or to propose optional courses of action which, if forced or persuaded on management, shift the singularity of responsibility of management to manage and perform satisfactorily.

Effectively to contribute to his abilities and knowledge, a board member should understand the business, that is, what it does and by what means and for what purpose. He must also be well read on the company, he should be analytical. He should require clarification where there is uncertainty. He should act for the purpose of satisfying himself that management is performing as expected, that the results are as forecast. He must be insistent on explanations for departures from the norm or the projected.

This is not to outdo management nor to disprove them. It is to satisfy himself that management – they being human too – did not overstate the prospects or underestimate the resources needed. He must satisfy himself that management is not overconfident, that it continues to be sound in its judgement, that it does not fail to react decisively to those changing circumstances I mentioned earlier.

Managements of business become possessive. Successful management may suffer from the seduction of success. This leads to latent resistance and the fear of interference. It leads to egotism in management, to a reluctance to disclose. The sense of possessiveness as an expression of pride and performance is commendable. It is less commendable when it is an expression of self flattery. Flattery is all very fine unless you inhale it.

So, an important contribution of the board is finding out to one's satisfied knowledge. Holding information tight to the chest by management is a paradox of behaviour be it arrogance or self-protection. The board should counter by showing management that the board is supportive, but does mean to know about its company and will not be left uncertain and in the dark.

I think the board director should be a good listener to colleagues and management. The timehogger who goes on and on is a bore in the board. A Churchill statement – he usually compresses the largest amount of words into the smallest amount of thought possible. That particular kind of director is a tribulation for the board and is a Chairman's problem to resolve. It is relevant to my earlier views on personal compatibility in those whom you would bring to the board to live with you.

The relationship between board and management is a reflection of board size, personality and strength of the Chief Executive and the Chairman, as well as the board character. Is it a directive or a supervisory board, or worst of all, is it only a nominal board? It is a subject I cannot develop in this short paper.

A wise board permits and requires management to manage, but makes sure to know what is happening. The character, personality and degree of involvement assumed by or required of the Chairman will influence board contribution, but should not diminish it.

The power to appoint a Chairman is permissive. Usually under the Articles, the directors appoint a Chairman of the Board, but this is primarily for the purpose of conducting their meetings and to take the chair at general meetings. Strictly speaking, there is no appointment as Chairman of the company.

The Chairman is the leader of the business, but not the operating and management leader. He and the Chief Executive are complementary one to the other working in mutual trust and harmony. The Chairman gives leadership through frequent communication with the Chief Executive. He gives leadership in board meetings. He is the public face of the company. He hold the board together. He protects management against antagonism or excessive criticism within the board or elsewhere. He ensures that management produces information which should be given to the board. He encourages management innovation and their ideas. He helps management with advice as to format and timing of presentations to the board.

He supports the Chief Executive in forceful decision making – remembering that piecemeal decisions are like being nibbled to death by ducks. He knows second line management and is selectively and carefully available to them – with the Chief Executive's knowledge and confidence.

He does not interfere, but he expects to be kept informed and he should also be an informer of board points of view and attitudes to the Chief Executive. There should be no shocks or surprises between the Chairman and the Chief Executive.

Like management, Chairmen can get ideas about their stature and this can become a difficult situation both for board and Chief Executive. There was the army office in which the office rules read:

1. The General is always right.
2. If the General is wrong, No. 1 applies.

That attitude obviously would make problems for the board director trying to hold his situation between the excessively authoritative Chairman and a resentful management.

Here is a list of the qualities of a Chairman, some of which all Chairmen possess, a lot of which all Chairmen should possess, but all of which it is unlikely any one Chairman does possess:

Judgment
Initiative
Integrity
Foresight
Energy
Ambition
Emotional stability
Dedication
Objectivity
Co-operation
Drive
Human relations skills
Decisiveness
Dependability
Fairness
Humour

The director has a changing role and times will change him. As I said earlier, it is not about privilege, but rather responsibility and accountability. Our brethren in the professions associated with business – especially the accountant and the lawyer – know that a new society means to hold themselves accountable for their actions and advises those who offer services upon which others may act.

As directors, our auditors require us to sign acceptances of responsibility for information given to or procured by them from our company records. Stock exchange regulations commit us to joint and several responsibility for published statements affecting actual and potential shareholders. All appointments to boards of banks in this country require prior approval by the Central Bank. There is a public voice about the neglect – real or not – of directors of failed companies. There is growing concern that there are circumstances in which directors of companies which have left employees, creditors and shareholders bereft can re-establish under another corporate name with no guarantee or obligation to perform better in the new venture than in the last.

If we fail as directors through inadequacy in the role, we are responsible for the losses of others and have breached the trust inherent in the position of director. We must be our own and each other's harshest critics of performance on the board. We have huge moral obligations to all those many elements which make our companies work. Our legal obligations may be expected to be more demanding in the future with punitive consequences for neglect, for not knowing, and for not having taken the time to find out.

There was a director with an inferiority complex who went to his doctor. After the usual questions, the doctor said, 'I can tell you positively you do not have an inferiority complex – you are just inferior'.

Mr Chairman and gentlemen, we should never relax against the risk of inferiority.

References

Abbreviations
DAA—Dublin Arch Diocese Archives
NA—National Archives
RTÉ A—RTÉ Archives
UCDA—UCD Archives

1   *The Irish Times*, 6 March 1976.
2   McCourt Papers—manuscript note, 9 May 1999.
3   *Leader*, 13 February 1904.
4   *Leader*, 27 February 1904.
5   O'Neill, *The Aghaderg Story*, pp. 8–9.
6   Foster, *Modern Ireland 1600–1972*, p. 431.
7   *The Irish Times*, 6 March 1976.
8   Harrington, *Kerry Landing, August 1922*, p. 50.
9   *Ibid.*, pp. 148–9.
10 *The Irish Times*, 6 March 1976.
11 *Ibid.*
12 *Ibid.*
13 *The Times*, 21 September 1972.
14 *The Irish Times*, 6 March 1976.
15 *Business and Finance*, 30 March 1978.
16 FIM Minutes, 28 April 1944, IBEC Archives.
17 McCourt Papers—unidentified newspaper extract.
18 *Ibid.*
19 *Irish Industrial Yearbook*, 1932.
20 FIM Minutes, 18 February 1938, IBEC Archives.

21 Memorandum of Association of FIM.
22 AGM Address, IBEC Archives.
23 *Monthly Review*, January 1935, quoted in O'Hagan & Foley, *The Confederation of Irish Industry: The First Fifty Years*.
24 NA CAB, 18 March 1932; BA D/T 6230.
25 *The Irish Times*, 6 September 1958.
26 Note in IBEC Archives.
27 *Irish Press*, 9 February 1944.
28 Bew & Patterson, *Seán Lemass and the Making of Modern Ireland 1945–66*, p. 20.
29 *Business and Finance*, 30 March 1978.
30 Bew & Patterson, p. 20.
31 *The Irish Times*, 12 February 1947.
32 Girvin, *Between Two Worlds*, 1989.
33 McCourt Papers.
34 *Ibid*.
35 *Ibid*.
36 AGM Address, IBEC Archives.
37 IBEC Archives.
38 McCourt Papers.
39 *Ibid*.
40 *Ibid*.
41 Minutes of SGM, 11 May 1948, IBEC Archives.
42 *Ibid*.
43 *Ibid*.
44 *Ibid*.
45 *Ibid*.
46 Newspaper extract, NA-P35b/45 (17).
47 NA-P35b/45 (16).
48 NA-P35b/45 (24).
49 *Ibid*.
50 Council Minutes, 30 June 1948, IBEC Archives.

51 NA-P35b/45 (17).
52 IBEC Archives.
53 McCourt Papers.
54 *Management*, March 1978.
55 *Ibid.*
56 UCDA – P356/75 (3).
57 *Ibid.*
58 AGM Minutes, 15 February 1949, IBEC Archives.
59 McCourt Papers—unidentified newspaper extract.
60 *Management*, 30 March 1978.
61 UCDA – P356/75 (4).
62 *Ibid.*
63 *Ibid.*
64 McCourt Papers.
65 *The Irish Times*, 1 June 1949.
66 *The Irish Times*, 31 May 1949.
67 Dáil Debates, 25 May 1949.
68 NA-P35b/51 (4).
69 *Ibid.*
70 *Ibid.*
71 *Ibid.*
72 NA-P35b/51 (5).
73 *Ibid.*
74 *Ibid.*
75 NA-SI4474.
76 *Ibid.*
77 *Ibid.*
78 *Ibid.*
79 *Ibid.*
80 Bew & Patterson, p. 59.
81 *Ibid.*, p. 58.
82 Girvin, p. 178.

83 Garvin, *Preventing the Future: Why was Ireland so poor for so long?*, p. 172.
84 *Ibid.*, p. 189.
85 Dáil Debates, 9 March 1950.
86 *Ibid.*
87 *Ibid.*
88 *Ibid.*, S. Collins TD.
89 *Ibid.*
90 *Ibid.*
91 *Ibid.*
92 *Ibid.*
93 Dáil Debates, 16 November 1950.
94 *Ibid.*
95 *Ibid.*
96 *Ibid.*
97 *Ibid.*
98 *Ibid.*
99 Girvin, p. 177.
100 NA-SI4474.
101 *Ibid.*
102 *Ibid.*
103 *Ibid.*
104 *Ibid.*
105 Dáil Debates, 12 July 1951.
106 *Ibid.*
107 *Business and Finance*, 30 March 1978.
108 *Management*, 30 March 1978.
109 *Ibid.*
110 *Business and Finance*, 30 March 1978.
111 *Ibid.*
112 *Ibid.*
113 *Business and Finance*, 30 March 1978.

114 McCourt Papers, letter dated 6 June 1951.
115 Plunkett, *P.J. Carroll & Co. Ltd., Dublin and Dundalk: a Retrospect on the Occasion of their 150th Anniversary.*
116 McCourt Papers—speech to Dublin Rotary Club, 21 September 1953.
117 *The Irish Times*, 27 November 1954.
118 Kenny, *In Good Company: Conversations with Irish Leaders*, pp. 311–12.
119 McCourt Papers.
120 *Ibid.*
121 *Ibid.*
122 *Ibid.*
123 *Ibid.*
124 *Ibid.*
125 *Ibid.*, letter from Gerald Sweetman, Minister for Finance, 29 October 1956.
126 McCourt Papers.
127 *Ibid.*
128 *Irish Independent*, 20 June 1955.
129 *Ibid.*, 21 June 1955.
130 *Ibid.*, 22 June 1955.
131 *Ibid.*, 24 June 1955.
132 *Ibid.*, 29 June 1955.
133 *Ibid.*, 30 June 1955.
134 *Ibid.*, 1 July 1955.
135 *Management*, March 1978.
136 *The Irish Times*, 26 November 1955.
137 McCourt Papers—unidentified newspaper extract.
138 *Business and Finance*, 30 March 1978.
139 *Management*, March 1978.
140 *Ibid.*
141 *Ibid.*

142 *Ibid.*
143 *The Irish Times*, 15 July 1959.
144 *The Irish Times*, 8 December 1959.
145 McCourt Papers, letter dated 9 July 1959.
146 *Ibid.*
147 *Management*, March 1978.
148 McCourt Papers—telegram dated 29 October 1962.
149 McCourt Papers—letter dated 26 October 1962.
150 McCourt Papers—letter dated 2 November 1962.
151 McCourt Papers.
152 Horgan, *Irish Media: a Critical History since 1922*, p. 80.
153 *Irish Press*, 1 January 1962.
154 McCourt Papers—unidentified newspaper extract.
155 *Ibid.*
156 *Ibid.*
157 *Ibid.*
158 *Ibid.*
159 *The Irish Times*, 22 February 1965.
160 *Sunday Press*, 2 December 1962.
161 *Irish Press*, 18 January 1963.
162 *Sunday Review*, 2 December 1962.
163 *Ibid.*
164 *Ibid.*
165 Dáil Debates, 11 December 1962.
166 *Business and Finance*, 30 March 1978.
167 RTÉ A, Minutes, 11 July 1963.
168 RTÉ A, Minutes, 16 July 1964.
169 RTÉ A, Minutes, 17 September 1964.
170 RTÉ A, Minutes, 10 January 1963.
171 NA-D/T S17461/63.
172 *Management*, March 1978.

173 Doolan, Dowling & Quinn, *Sit Down and be Counted: the Cultural Evolution of a Television Station*, p. 33.
174 RTÉ A, Minutes, 6 June 1963.
175 Radio interview.
176 *Ibid.*
177 Doolan, Dowling & Quinn, p. 36.
178 NA-S3532 C/63, letter dated 26 September 1962.
179 *Ibid.*
180 NA-S3532, memorandum, 4 January 1963.
181 RTÉ A, Minutes, 28 November 1963.
182 *Ibid.*
183 *Ibid.*
184 *Ibid.*
185 NA-S3532/C/63.
186 McCourt interview with John Horgan, quoted in Horgan, *Seán Lemass: the Enigmatic Patriot.*
187 *The Irish Times*, 1 January 2002.
188 DAA, letter dated 12 December 1963.
189 DAA.
190 DAA, letter dated 18 December 1963.
191 McCourt Papers—note prepared in January 1996 by Kevin McCourt for Fr J. Dunn.
192 *Ibid.*
193 *Ibid.*
194 NA-S3532/D/95.
195 *Ibid.*
196 *Ibid.*
197 *Ibid.*
198 RTÉ A, Minutes, 23 January 1964.
199 RTÉ A, Minutes, 14 January 1965.
200 RTÉ A, Minutes, 17 June 1965.
201 RTÉ A, Minutes, 6 October 1965.

202 *Ibid.*
203 RTÉ A.
204 RTÉ A, Minutes, 15 December 1965.
205 RTÉ A, Minutes, 30 March 1966.
206 RTÉ A, Minutes, 5 January 1966.
207 RTÉ A, Minutes, 20 April 1966.
208 McCourt Papers.
209 McCourt Papers—letter dated 25 April 1966.
210 McCourt Papers—statement, 24 May 1966.
211 McCourt Papers—letter dated 30 May 1966.
212 McCourt Papers—letter dated 25 June 1966.
213 Andrews, E. *This is My Life*, p. 239.
214 McCourt papers—note prepared in January 1996 by Kevin McCourt for Fr J. Dunn.
215 Letter to *Irish Press*, 27 May 1966.
216 *Ibid.*
217 RTÉ A, Minutes, 25 May 1966.
218 McCourt Papers—Rugheimer interview with John Horgan, 23 March 1995.
219 RTÉ A, Minutes, 21 July 1965.
220 *Ibid.*
221 RTÉ A, Minutes, 30 March 1966.
222 Radio interview.
223 RTÉ A, Minutes, 20 April 1966.
224 *Sunday Press*, 13 February 1966.
225 Byrne, *To Whom it Concerns*, p. 74.
226 *Ibid.*, p. 75.
227 *The Irish Times*, 14 February 1966.
228 Byrne, p. 79.
229 *Ibid.*, pp. 76–7.
230 Cooney, *John Charles McQuaid: Ruler of Catholic Ireland*, p. 384.

231 Horgan, *Broadcasting and Public Life: RTÉ News and Current Affairs 1926–1977*, p. 31.
232 RTÉ A, Minutes, 16 February 1966.
233 Byrne, p. 87.
234 *Ibid.*, p. 95.
235 RTÉ A, Minutes, 30 March 1966.
236 Horgan, p. 32.
237 Gay Byrne interview with the author.
238 Dáil Debates, 12 October 1966.
239 Andrews, C.S., *Man of No Property*, p. 271.
240 *Ibid.*
241 *Management*, March 1978.
242 *Irish Independent*, 13 March 1969.
243 McCourt Papers—letter dated 13 March 1969.
244 *The Irish Times*, 4 October 1966.
245 *Ibid.*
246 *Ibid.*
247 *Ibid.*
248 *The Irish Times*, 5 October 1966.
249 Muiris MacConghail interview with the author.
250 Dáil Debates, 12 October 1966.
251 NA-98/6/19, Childers to Lynch, 4 December 1966.
252 Radio interview.
253 Dáil Debates, 20 April 1967.
254 *Ibid.*
255 Andrews, C.S., p. 277.
256 Doolan, Dowling & Quinn, Appendix III, letter to the Taoiseach, 18 April 1967.
257 Radio interview.
258 Doolan, Dowling & Quinn, Appendix III.
259 RTÉ A, Minutes, 5 May 1967.
260 *Ibid.*

261 Horgan, p. 52.
262 RTÉ Programme Policy Committee, Minutes, 9 November 1967.
263 NA-98/2/28.
264 Tom O'Dea in the *Irish Press*, 17 February 1968.
265 Andrews, C.S., p. 278.
266 Doolan, Dowling & Quinn, p. 124.
267 *Ibid.*, p. 111.
268 Muiris MacConghail interview with the author.
269 Andrews, C.S., p. 278.
270 *Ibid.*
271 RTÉ A, statement dated 16 February 1968.
272 McCourt Papers—unidentified newspaper extract.
273 McCourt Papers—unidentified newspaper extract.
274 *The Irish Times*, 21 February 1968.
275 McCourt Papers—unidentified newspaper extract.
276 Andrews, C.S. p. 280.
277 Muiris MacConghail interview with the author.
278 Radio interview.
279 *Management*, March 1978.
280 McCourt Papers.
281 Doolan, Dowling & Quinn, p. 32.
282 McCourt Papers—letter dated 21 December 1967.
283 Tom Hardiman interview with the author.
284 Gay Byrne interview with the author.
285 McCourt Papers.
286 McCourt Papers—unidentified newspaper extract, June 1969.
287 *Business and Finance*, 30 March 1978.
288 McCourt Papers—unidentified newspaper extract, April 1968.
289 *Ibid.*

290 *Ibid.*
291 *Ibid.*
292 *The Irish Times*, 26 February 1969.
293 *International Management*, November 1971.
294 *Ibid.*
295 *Business and Finance*, 28 February 1969.
296 *Fortune*, July 1969.
297 *The Irish Times*, 23 August 1969.
298 *The Irish Times*, 26 November 1969.
299 McCourt Papers—miscellaneous unidentified newspaper extracts.
300 *Business and Finance*, 19 December 1969.
301 *Ibid.*
302 *Ibid.*
303 *Ibid.*
304 *Fortune*, July 1969.
305 *The Times*, 7 January 1970.
306 *Ibid.*
307 Marketing communications, July 1970.
308 McCourt Papers.
309 *Ibid.*
310 *Irish Press*, 30 April 1970.
311 *Ibid.*
312 Ivor Kenny, *Leaders: Conversations wth Irish Chief Executives*, p. 10.
313 McCourt Papers.
314 *The Sunday Times*, 2 May 1971.
315 *Sunday Independent*, 7 November 1971.
316 McCourt Papers—letter to the Managing Director of John Dewar and Sons, 21 June 1972.
317 *Business and Finance*, 30 March 1978.
318 *The Irish Times*, 18 October 1972.

References 211

319 *Business and Finance*, 17 November 1972.
320 Richard Burrows interview with the author.
321 As told to the author by Conal McCourt.
322 *Business and Finance*, December 1974.
323 McCourt Papers—speech to IDG Management Conference, 5 October 1977.
324 *Business and Finance*, 30 March 1978.
325 IDG Management Conference, 5 October 1977.
326 *Management*, March 1978.
327 McCourt Papers—letter from McCourt to O'Reilly, 3 April 1978.
328 *The Irish Times*, 31 March 1978.
329 *The Irish Times*, 24 May 1989.
330 *Management*, March 1978.
331 RTÉ A, Minutes, 13 May 1965.
332 Justin Keating interview with the author.
333 NA D/T S11987B, memorandum to the Government, 15 February 1947.
334 McCourt Papers.
335 McCourt Papers—unidentified newspaper extract.
336 *The Irish Times*, 18 March 1976.
337 *The Irish Times*, 26 April 1977.
338 *The Irish Times*, 24 March 1977.
339 *Ibid.*
340 *Business and Finance*, 7 February 1978.
341 *Ibid.*
342 *Ibid.*
343 *Irish Press*, 13 January 1978.
344 McCourt Papers—undated extract from *Magill* magazine.
345 *The Irish Times*, 18 January 1978.
346 Hogan, *A History of Irish Steel*.
347 *The Irish Times*, 3 October 1981.

348 *The Irish Times*, 6 November 1981.
349 Dáil Debates, 29 June 1982.
350 As told to the author by Liam Coughlan.
351 *The Irish Times*, 28 June 1983.
352 *The Irish Times*, 30 June 1983.
353 *The Irish Times*, 21 September 1983.
354 *The Irish Times*, 23 June 1984.
355 *The Irish Times*, 9 November 1984.
356 *The Irish Times*, 14 June 1985.
357 *The Irish Times*, 15 June 1985.
358 *The Irish Times*, 2 August 1985.
359 *The Irish Times*, 16 August 1985.
360 Dáil Debates, 17 December 1985.
361 Seanad Debates, 19 December 1985.
362 *The Irish Times*, 6 March 1976.
363 McCourt Papers—IOD Address, 12 November 1986. See Appendix, page 188.
364 *Ibid.*
365 *Ibid.*
366 *Dundalk Democrat*, 5 October 1957.
367 McCourt Papers—unidentified newspaper extract.
368 *The Irish Times*, 6 March 1976.
369 McCourt Papers—unidentified newspaper extract.
370 Michael Smurfit interview with the author.
371 Dermot Desmond interview with the author.
372 *Management*, March 1978.
373 *Ibid.*
374 *Ibid.*
375 Note to the author.
376 McCourt Papers.
377 *The Irish Times*, 6 March 1976.
378 *Ibid.*

379 McCourt Papers—unidentified newspaper extract.
380 Letter to Melissa McCourt, 13 April 1988.
381 *The Irish Times*, 18 January 1965.

Selected Bibliography

Andrews, C.S., *Man of No Property*, Cork: Mercier Press, 1982.

Andrews, E., *This is My Life: the Autobiography of Eamonn Andrews*, London: MacDonald, 1963.

Bew, P. & Patterson, H., *Seán Lemass and the Making of Modern Ireland, 1945–66*, Dublin: Gill & MacMillan, 1982.

Byrne, G., *To Whom it Concerns*, Dublin: Torc Books, 1972.

Cooney, J., *John Charles McQuaid: Ruler of Catholic Ireland*, Dublin: The O'Brien Press, 1999.

Doolan, L., Dowling, J. & Quinn B., *Sit Down and Be Counted: the Cultural Evolution of a Television Station*, Dublin: Wellington Publishers, 1969.

Foster, R.F., *Modern Ireland 1600–1972*, London: Penguin Books, 1989.

Garvin, T., *Preventing the Future: Why was Ireland so Poor for so Long?*, Dublin: Gill & MacMillan, 2004.

Girvin, B., *Between Two Worlds: Politics and Economy in Independent Ireland*, Dublin: Gill & MacMillan, 1989.

Harrington, N.C., *Kerry Landing, August 1922: an Episode of the Civil War*, Dublin: Anvil Books, 1992.

Hogan, S., *A History of Irish Steel*, Dublin: Gill & MacMillan, 1980.

Horgan, J., *Broadcasting and Public Life: RTÉ News and Current Affairs 1926–1977*, Dublin: Four Courts Press, 2004.

Horgan, J., *Irish Media: a Critical History since 1922*, London: Routledge, 2001.

Horgan, J., *Seán Lemass: the Enigmatic Patriot*, Dublin: Gill & MacMillan, 1997.

Kenny, I., *Leaders: Conversations with Irish Chief Executives*, Cork: Oak Tree Press, 2001.

Kenny, I., *In Good Company: Conversations with Irish Leaders*, Dublin: Gill & MacMillan, 1987.

MacSharry, R. & White P., *The Making of the Celtic Tiger: the Inside Story of Ireland's Boom Economy*, Cork: Mercier Press, 2000.

O'Hagan, J.W. & Foley, G.J., *The Confederation of Irish Industry: the First Fifty Years, 1932–1982*, Dublin: Confederation of Irish Industry, 1982.

O'Neill, G., *The Aghaderg Story: a History of Gaelic Games and Culture in the Parish of Aghaderg 1903–1984*, Ireland: Aghaderg GAA Club, 1984.

Plunkett, J., *P.J. Carroll & Co., Ltd., Dublin and Dundalk: a Retrospect on the Occasion of their 150th Anniversary*, Dublin: P.J. Carroll & Co., 1974.

Index

A
Advertising Press Club 62, 181
Aghaderg 7
Ahern, Bertie 176
Aiken, Frank 110
Algemene Bank Nederland (ANB) 172–73
Alton Box Board Company 174
Andrews, Eamonn 72, 73, 76, 77, 79, 80, 83–4, 102, 171
    resigns over Rugheimer campaign 90–92
    reactions to 95–6
    response to Kevin McCourt 94
    thwarting John Charles McQuaid 86
Andrews, Grainne 92
Andrews, Dr C.S. (Tod) 109, 117, 120
    arrival at RTÉ 101
    regarding Garda Special Branch programme 115–6
    regarding Kevin McCourt 102–3
    Vietnam coverage debate 111
Angler's Rest, Headford 183
Anglesea Tennis Club, Ballsbridge 12
Anglo-Irish Trade Agreement 1938 19, 23–4, 136
Annual Convention of the National Licensed Beverage Association 135

Argosy Library *see* McCourt, John (Seán)
Attlee, Clement 28
Aung, Myo 68

B
BBC 73
Ballyseedy 8–9
Ballyvarley 7
Baltimore Technologies 175–76
Banbridge 5, 7, 10
    first hurling club 6
Barry, Michael 79
Baum, Fr Gregory 85
Beddy, J.P. 35, 39
    IDA proposals 51–2
Beggar's Bush barracks 13
Biafra state 114
Black and Tans 8
Blackrock College 11, 184
Blackrock R.F.C. 183
Blaney, Neal 171
Blythe, Ernest 73
Bonner, Ted 150
Bord Fáilte 172
Bord na Móna 101
Brennan, Joseph 91
British Distillers Company 151
British National Coal Board 161
British Steel 154
Broadcasting Act 1960 73
Bronfman, Charles 142
Browne TD, Dr Noël 76, 115

Brugha, Ruaidhri 88, 96
Bruton, John 162, 163, 165
   pays tribute to Kevin McCourt 166
Burke, Edmund 94
Burns, Robert 56
Burrows, Richard 138, 144, 147–48, 175
Business and Finance 130, 158
Byrne, Gay 101, 114, 135
   Late Late Show 89–90
      controversial guests 99–100
      'the Bishop and the Nightie' 97–9
   pays tribute to Kevin McCourt 123–4
Byrne, John 166

C

C.E. Macauleys 12
C.I.É. 101
Campbell, Mrs Patrick 125
Canadian Broadcasting Corporation 79
Capital Investment Advisory Committee 63
Carroll, Charles 56–7
   see also P.J. Carroll
Carroll, Don 69, 137
Carroll, James 55–7, 68
   see also P.J. Carroll
   regarding Kevin McCourt's departure 70
   regarding tobacco duty 57–8
Carroll, Patrick Joseph 57
Carroll, Vincent 56–7
   see also P.J. Carroll
Carroll, Vincent Stannus 57
Carroll, Walter 56–7

   see also P.J. Carroll
Casement, Roger 9
Castleknock College, Dublin 70
Catholic Television Interim Committee 85
Charrington, Bass 142
Chartered Institute of Secretaries 15, 62, 189
Childers, Erskine 14, 109, 110
Christian Brothers 10
Civil War 9
Clann na Banna 6
Clinton, Bill 176
Clinton, Mark 171
Clonmore 13
Clover Meats 159
Cluskey, Frank 119
College of Commerce, Rathmines 11–12
Colley, George 172
Collins, Michael 8–9, 96
Commission for Justice and Peace 171
Communist Party 115
Confederation of British Industry 32
Confederation of Irish Industry 140
Congested Districts Board 5
Connolly Shoes Limited, Dundalk
   see Folwell, Mr
Connolly, St John 31
Conradh na Gaeilge 96
Control of Manufacturers Act 1932
   see Lemass, Seán
Control of Manufacturers Act 1934 17
Cook, Archie 130, 136
Corás Tráchtála 44, 63
Cork Distilleries Co. Ltd 126

Cosgrove, Liam 76
Costello, John A. 24, 28, 33, 54
Coughlan, Liam 159, 166
Council of Gorta 171
Cox, Arthur 18, 55, 60
    joins P.J. Carroll 57
Crichton, Aleck 126, 129
Cripps, Stanford 28
Cronkite, Walter 110
Crookes, Gearoid 184
Crossley Surveys 134
Culleton, Jim 186
Cumann na nGaedhael 47

D

Dancel, John *see* McCourt, Kevin
de Valera, Éamon 17, 73, 96, 103
de Vere White, Terence 119
Department of Education 87
Department of External Affairs 80–81
Department of Finance 73
Department of Industry and Commerce 17
Department of Post and Telegraphs 72, 87
Desmond, Dermot 175, 176
Dichter, Ernest 134
Dillon, Dave 129, 132
Dillon, James 28
Dodd, Fr Romuald 86
Dorchester Hotel, London 68
Drumcondra 12
Dublin Guards 9
Dublin Industrial Development Association 15
Dublin Rotary Club 21–2, 57
Dublin Theatre Festival 182
Dublin United Tramways 11
Dublin Vocational Education Committee 61
Duffy, Senator Luke 35, 50
Duke of Wellington 194
Dulanty, Mr J. 28
Dun Laoghaire 10
Dundalk Democrat 170
Dundalk Engineering Works Ltd 170
Dunganstown, Co. Wexford 80
Dunn, Fr Joseph 86, 171

E

Eason & Son 35
Easter Rising 1916 8–9, 96
Economic War 23
Economist 192
Edward Dillon & Co. 131
Edward Gottlieb and Associates 134
Elswick Hopper bicycle 11
Emerson, Ralph Waldo 194
European Coal and Steel Community (ECSC) 154
European Commission 158, 175
    allows state aid for steel companies 162–64
European Economic Community (EEC) 140, 165
    Ireland's accession to 154
    steelworkers' fund 165
Evening Herald 140
Evening Press 11
Expo' 70, Osaka 132–33

F

Federated Union of Employers 34–5
Federation of Irish Manufacturers (FIM) 43, 140
    AGM 1947 23–31

AGM 1949 34
  eleventh annual general meeting 16
  principal objectives 15–16
  regarding new Trade Agreement 29–30
  row with NAIDA 30
Fenit pier 9
Ferrco 155–56
Fianna Fáil 16, 18, 41, 48, 53, 157, 172
  anger at IDA 35–6
Fine Gael 33, 41, 76, 103
First World War 133
Fitzgerald, Alexis 33
FitzGerald, Garret 166
Fitzgerald, Gene 157
Fitzwilton 143
Fóir Teoranta 172
Folwell, Mr
  Connolly Shoes Limited, Dundalk 27
Foreign Trade Committee 44

G
Gael Linn 88
Gaelic Athletic Association 5, 6
  Central Council 7
Gaelic League 5, 8, 89
  objectives 7
Gallagher, Matt 115
Garda Special Branch 115
Garvey, Michael 97, 115, 117, 118, 120
General Election 1944 18
General Election 1948 153
General Election 1953 50
Government Information Bureau 81–2
Gray, E.J. 140

Great Northern Railway 170
Gresham Hotel 25, 27
Griffin, Noel 143
Guinness, Henry 57

H
Hamill, John 42
Hardiman, Tom 80, 123
Harrods 185
Haughey, Charles J. 84, 103, 108, 164
Heffernan, Gerry 155–56
Hibernian Insurance 174
Hibernian Life Association 174–75
Hilliard, Michael 84
Hogan, G.P.S. 154
Home Rule Bill 5
Horgan, John 73, 114
Hunter Douglas 69
  see also Soonenberg, Henry

I
Industrial Credit Company 35
Industrial Credit Corporation 52
Industrial Development Authority (IDA)
  see also Lemass, Seán; McGilligan, Patrick
  core complaints about 45
  first task of 47–8
  functions of 33–4
  interim report 42–3, 44–5
  launch of 40
  low morale 51–2
Institute of Directors 167
International School, The Hague 70
Investment Bank of Ireland 136
Irish Catholic 98

Irish Council of the European
    Movement 140
Irish Distillers Group 139, 141, 142
    AGM 1976 147
    control of Old Bushmills 144–45
    Midleton plant 147, 151
    relationship with Seagrams
        143–44
    strike in 1974 145–46
Irish Glass Bottle Group 136
Irish Independent 65, 140
Irish Management Institute 61, 177
Irish Parliamentary Party
    demise of 8
Irish Press 29, 35, 95, 137, 140, 158
Irish Red Cross Society
    Irish Freedom from Hunger
        Campaign 171
Irish Republican Brotherhood 9
Irish Steel Holdings Ltd 152, 166
    European Commission letter
        158–59
    economic difficulties 160–63
    'go it alone' plan 156–57
    strike 1977 157
    trading history 153–54
    voluntary redundancy scheme
        155
Irish Stock Exchange 173
Irish Times, The 140, 149–50, 159,
        161, 165, 186–87
    'Montrose emotion' 119–120
    '*Quid Nunc*' column 64–5
    'Run for Cover' 107
    'The Bishop and the Nightie' 98
Irish Transport and General
        Workers Union 73
Irish Volunteers 8
Irvine, John 115, 122
ISPAT International 166

J

Jameson Distiller, Bow Street 127,
    128–29
Jefferson Smurfit Group 172,
    173–74
John Jameson & Son 126
    Jameson North American Blend
        135–36
    Paddy 134
    Power's 134
    Tullamore Dew 134
John Power & Son Ltd 126
John Power Distillery, John's Lane
    128–29
Joseph Seagrams & Sons 141–44

K

Kapp & Peterson 182
Kavanagh, P.J. 24, 28
Keating, Justin 152
Kennedy Crowley and Co. 12
Kennedy, Mrs Jacqueline 81
Kennedy, President John F. 80
Kenny, Professor Ivor 177
Killanin, Lord 175
Kilroy, Howard 172
    pays tribute to Kevin McCourt
        186
Kipping, Sir Norman 32, 68–9

L

La Chassotte, Switzerland 70
Labour Court 157, 165
Labour Party 50
Lacha, Daithi 95, 117
Lady Wicklow 9
Larkin TD, James 40–1
Late Late Show see Byrne, Gay
Lawrence, T.E. 10
Leader 6

Ledwidge, Frances 182
Lemass, Seán 31, 55, 153, 170
　anger at IDA 35–6, 46–50
　Dáil speech 41–2
　'pompous ass' 51
　proposes new role 53
　Control of Manufacturers Act 1932 17–18
　criticises Telefís Éireann 81–3, 86–7, 108–9
　Industrial Efficiency Bill 46
　Memorandum on Full Economic Policy 19
　relationship with Kevin McCourt 19–20
Lentin, Louis 97
Life Association Ireland 174–75
Liston S.C., T.K. 120
Little, Arthur D. 130, 157
Local Defence Force 12
London Association of Accountants 15
London Stock Exchange 173, 176
Loughbrickland 7
Lownes, Victor 99–100
Lynch, Jack 109, 114, 157, 172, 183

M

MacBride, Seán
　Minister for External Affairs 28, 46, 52
MacConghail, Muiris 108, 115, 120–21
　suspends himself 116
MacCuarta, Séamus Dall 5–6
Machiavelli 194
Macy's Department Store, New York 185
Magill 158–59
Management 148

McCann, Hugh 114
McCourt, Brendan 10
McCourt, Declan 13, 70
　regarding his father 186
McCourt, Deirdre 13, 70
McCourt, Dermot 10
McCourt, Germaine 13, 70
McCourt, Irene 10
McCourt, John (Seán) 5–6, 10
　dissatisfaction with GAA 6–7
　set up Argosy Library 10
　sues parish priest 8
McCourt, Kevin Colum
　Algemene Bank Nederland appointment 172–73
　as public speaker 20–21, 182
　at Advertising Press Club 62, 181–82
　at Chartered Institute of Secretaries 62
　at Social Study Conference, Dundalk 60
　Baltimore Technologies appointment 175–76
　becomes a father 13
　becomes an accountant 11–12
　birth date 5
　Capital Investment Advisory Committee appointment 63
　Córas Tráchtála appointment 63
　Council of Gorta appointment 171
　death 186
　demanding leader 180
　denouncing NAIDA 31
　describes Gunnar Rugheimer 79–80
　describes Seán Lemass 19–20, 31
　Dundalk Engineering Works Ltd appointment 170–71

education, importance of 182
'Education Management' 61–2
first job 11
Fóir Teoranta appointment 172
fly fishing 183
marriage 12 *see also* McMahon, Margaret (Peggy)
Harmony Cottage 183
Hibernian Life appointment 174
Hunter Douglas appointment 69–71, 76, 172
IDA appointment 35
   resigns from 53–5
Irish Steel Holdings Ltd (ISH) appointment 152
   AGM 1981 160
   'go it alone' plan 156–57
   Haulbowline expansion bid 158–59
   proposes redundancies 164–65
      appeals to workers 166
   resigns 166
   stands up to Ian McGregor 161
   voluntary redundancy scheme 155
   writes to *Irish Times* 162
Jefferson Smurfit Group appointment 173–74
joins LDF 12–13
Kerry memories 8–10
language courses 182–83
Life Association Ireland 174
lifelong friends 184
love for Ireland 179
love for Italy 183
loves being a director 167–68

   non-executive qualities 168–70
moves to Dublin 10–11
P.J Carroll & Co. appointment 56
   'Behind the Smoke Screen' 57
   business trips 64–8
      as John Dancel 65–7
   export markets critical 62–3
   'The Urgency of Exports' 63–4
   improving sales 58–9
   'The High Cost of Not Advertising' 59
Peterson Tennant appointment 182
protecting industry and tariffs 22–3
Radio Éireann appointment 72–7, 171
   7 Days troubles 116–20
   Biafra coverage trouble 114–5, 118
   deals with criticisms 81–4
      Archbishop John Charles McQuaid 84–6
   defending *Late Late Show* 100–01
   Garda Special Branch programme 115–6, 118
   housing difficulties 77
   Kennedy's visit 80–81
   NUJ dispute 78
      further disagreements 106–9
   political accusations 103–9
      regarding Tod Andrews 103

Rugheimer controversy
   88–90
      upset as Eamonn Andrews
         resigns 92–5
   Telefís Scoile 87
   'the Bishop and the Nightie'
      scandal 98–9
   Vietnam coverage debate
      110–13
   won't renew contract 113–4
      leaves early 120–21
      reflects on experience
         121–22
      tributes paid to him
         122–25
regarding his father 5–6
secretary of FIM 14–15, 31–2, 54
   regarding 1938 Trade
      Agreement 25–7
   regarding 1948 Agreement
      29–30
sense of style 181
Sunday Independent business
   articles 139
   NUJ dispute 140
United Distillers of Ireland
      appointment 126
   Bow Street headquarters 128
   cracking US market 133–35
      'Irish Distiller's Klondike'
         144
   Expo' 70 132–33
   first report 128
   making changes 129–31
   new duty arrangements 132
   Old Bushmills acquisition
      144–45
   press reception 127–28
   retires 147–48
      tributes paid 148–50

   strike 1974 145–47
   sums up achievements
      150–51
   'what constitutes success'
      interview 177–78
   working hours 180
McCourt, Pamela 13, 21, 70
   regarding her father 178
McEvoy, P.L. 23, 29, 30
   regarding IDA 34
McGilligan, Patrick 28, 43–4
   sceptical of IDA 36–9
McGrath, Patrick 137
McGregor, Ian 161
McGuinness, Jim 116, 117, 118
McKinley, Joseph 57
McMahon, Margaret (Peggy) 12,
   64, 69, 92
   Deirdre Designs 185
   describes husband 75–6
   illness 186
McPolin, Dean 7–8
McQuaid, Fr John Charles 11,
   98–100
   criticises Telefís Éireann 81,
      84–6, 115
Messrs. Cooper Brothers and Co.,
   Chartered Accountants 137,
   138
Midleton Distillery 126
   Midleton Reserve 139
Mitchell, Peat Marwick 138
Morris, Archbishop Thomas 85–6
Morrissey, Daniel
   Minister for Industry and
      Commerce 28
   regarding IDA 33–4, 39–40
      introducing Second Stage
         47–8
Murphy, James 126

Murphy, Professor Michael 35

N
na Gopaleen, Myles 74–5
Napoleon 123
Nasdaq 176
National Advertising Conference 1952
  Kevin McCourt speaks at 59–60
National Agricultural and Industrial Development Association 15
  row with FIM 30–31
National Union of Journalists 106–7
  dispute regarding Kevin McCourt's business articles 140
  Journalists on Strike 78
  Vietnam coverage debate 111
Nazis 12
Norton, William
  Minister for Social Welfare 28

O
O'Brien, John 34–5
O'Broin, Leon 72–3
O'Driscoll, T.J. 172
O'Faoláin, Tomás *see* O'Sullivan, Terry
O'Farachíain, Riobárd
  pays tribute to Kevin McCourt 124–25
O hAnracháin, Padraig 81–3
O'Hehir, Michael 117
O'Higgins, T.F 49
  criticises RTÉ coverage 103–4
  writes about Kevin McCourt 187
O'Kelly, Sean T. 88
O'Malley, Desmond 157, 160
O'Morain, Donall 88, 89–90
O'Reilly, Frank 126, 127, 129, 140, 143, 147
  tribute paid by Kevin McCourt 148–49
O'Reilly, Michael 140
O'Reilly, Reggie 132, 135, 136
O'Reilly, Tony 143
  pays tribute to Kevin McCourt 186
O'Sullivan, Terry 68
  'Dubliner's Diary' 11
Old Bushmills Distillery 127, 142, 144, 151
Organisation for European Economic Co-operation 42

P
P.J. Carroll & Co. 136, 137
  beginnings of 56
  Carroll's Number 1 68
  'Emerald Glen' 56
  invite Kevin McCourt onboard 55
  'Mick McQuaid' 56
  record profits 1969 70
  reduction in profits 1951 58
  'Sweet Afton' 56
Paisley, Reverend Ian 144
Parnell, Charles Stuart 8
Pearse, Patrick 96
  'The Nature of Freedom' 9
Pembroke Cricket Club 183
Peterson Tennant 182
Phelan, Tommy *see* O'Sullivan, Terry
Plunkett, James 56
Pope John XXIII 85
Power, James 126
presidential election 1966 103

R
Radio Éireann Authority 72, 83, 118–19, 121, 152

Radio Telefís Éireann 73
   7 Days 115, 118–19
   An Nuacht 88, 95
   Ceamara na Cruinne 90
   Division 108
   Gorta at Work 171
   Insurrection 97
   Late Late Show 89–90, 117–18
   Leargas 90
   President Kennedy's visit 80
   Programme Policy Committee 114
   Quicksilver 117
   Radharc series 86
      Gorta Gives a Dam 171
   'Thursday Topic' 83
   versus Sean Lemass 83
Ranelagh 10
Redmond, John 8
Reynolds, Albert 161
Roadstone 184
Robinson, Ronnie 129
Roche, Tom 184
Rooney, Fran 175, 176
Roth, Edward 73, 76, 77, 82
Ruane, Professor J.B. 87
Rugheimer, Gunnar 79
   controversial appointment 80
   campaign against 88–90
Ryan, Clem 128, 129, 135
Ryan, John A. 137
Ryan, Bishop Tom 97

S
Salinger, Pierre 81
Savage, Gene 132
Second Programme for Economic Expansion 1964 87
Second Vatican Council 85
Second World War 18–19, 68
Shannon Scheme 47

Shelbourne Hotel 109, 120, 181
Small, Mary Christina (Minnie) 5
Smith, Con 140
Smurfit Snr, Jefferson 172
Smurfit, Michael 174, 186
Soonenberg, Henry 68–9
Staines airplane disaster 140–41
Stanley, John 162
Stephen's Green Club 60
Sugrue, Patrick 10
Summerfield, F.M. 14, 27
Sunday Independent 139, 140
Sunday Press 97
Sunday Review 75
Sunday Times 139
Suntory 133
Sweetman, Michael 140

T
Telefís Éireann *see* Radio Telefís Éireann
Telefís Scoile 87
Telstar 81
Thatcher, Margaret 161
Thornley, David 96, 120–21
Time Industries Inc. 174
Tralee 5, 9
   Clonmore Terrace 13
Treaty of Paris 154
Trevaskis, Brian 100
Twain, Mark 179

U
Ui Ceallaigh, Filis Bean 88, 97
United Distillers of Ireland 126–27, 131, 136, 137–38, 151, 171
   name change 139
United Nations 171
University College, Cork 35

W
Walsh, J.J. 35
War of Independence 9
Waterford Glass 136, 137–38, 143
Watkins, Kathleen 135
Webb, Ivan 140
White House 80
White, Jack 82

Williams, Edmund 172, 175
World Food Congress 171
World Steel Conference 161

Y
Yeats, W.B. 8
Yogman, Jack 141–42, 147